Terri Tanielian, Caroline Batka, Lisa S. Meredith

Bridging Gaps in Mental Health (

Lessons Learned from the Welcome Back Veterans Initia

RAND HEALTH

Sponsored by the Robert R. McCormick Foundation

Figure and Tables

Figure

Tables

tions around the United States to create and implement programs focused on addressing the mental health needs of returning veterans and their families (see Table S.1).

In 2010, the McCormick Foundation contracted RAND to serve as the performance-monitoring center for WBV. In 2014, RAND released a report on Phase I of WBV's activities and lessons learned. This report builds on the earlier one by including an update on Phase 2 of WBV activities (between 2013 and 2015), while also placing these activities within the larger context of the nation's evolving systems of care that address mental health issues for veterans and their families. During both phases, RAND's role was to collect data from grantees quarterly on their activities and progress, including information on the individuals receiving clinical services, partnership development, outreach and dissemination activities, education and training efforts, and challenges and goals. The RAND team also conducted quarterly calls with each grantee to discuss program activities and progress.

Notable Phase II Activities

In Phase II of the initiative, grantees focused their services on maximizing impact and aligning with the WBV aim of establishing sustainable programs that support the mental health needs of service members, veterans, and families through public-private partnerships. Activities were concentrated in four areas: delivering clinical services, training, raising awareness, and creating referral networks.

Delivering clinical services. Since 2010, WBV grantees provided clinical services to a total of 915 active component service members, 3,771 veterans, 901 reserve and guard members, and 5,146 family members in the form of screening, referrals, and treatment or care. Four of the seven WBV sites deliver clinical care services directly to veterans and their families through individual or group therapy. (Grantees use evidence-based or evidence-informed therapeutic interventions in clinical services for service members, veterans, and families.) Two other sites offer nonmedical evidence-based or evidence-informed support services to families.

In recognition of the myriad of issues that veterans and their families face, sites developed clinical services for a range of clinical issues that impact service members, veterans, and their families, including PTSD, depression, military sexual trauma, traumatic grief, and anxiety. Supplementing specialized options offered in the U.S. Department of Defense, VA, and community systems of care, grantees have offered clinical services and training courses specifically oriented toward such issues as military sexual trauma, TBI, female veterans, homeless veterans, and military families.

Training: Expanding the provider pool, enhancing competence. WBV grantees' training has focused on expanding the pool of providers who can deliver culturally competent mental health care to service members, veterans, and their families. As reported at the June 2014 all-grantee meeting, the WBV initiative rivals VA training

Table S.1
Welcome Back Veterans Programs

Program	Site	Focus	Special Programs
Emory's Veterans Program	Emory University, Atlanta, Ga.	Offers free clinical treatment for post-9/11 veterans and their family members in Georgia and the southeastern United States.	With WBV support, developed program to train community-based mental health providers to offer evidence-based treatments.
Duke University Veteran Culture and Clinical Competencies	Duke University, Durham N.C.	Training and supplemental implementation activities for community-based providers.	Developed intensive training models for organizations of providers, such as a model that trains 4–8 providers over six months.
Red Sox Home Base Program	Massachusetts General Hospital, Boston, Mass.	Offers treatment for PTSD and traumatic brain injury (TBI) among post-9/11 service members, veterans, and families in New England.	Created Home Base Institute, which will serve as a training hub for community providers.
Nathanson Family Resilience Center (NFRC)	University of California, Los Angeles, Los Angeles, Calif.	Family-centered approach to clinical services and education.	Developed Families OverComing Under Stress (FOCUS) Prevention Program that promotes resilience among military families. UCLA NFRC has leveraged technology to target military families who need care and to deliver training courses.
Road Home Program	Rush University, Chicago, Ill.	Provides clinical services for post-9/11 service members, veterans, and their families. Also offers training, military culture competency for health care providers and family caregivers.	Aims to use the FOCUS and TeleFOCUS models, developed at NFRC, to train community providers that serve military families.
Military Support Programs and Networks	University of Michigan Depression Center, Ann Arbor, Mich.	Offers mental health research and peer support programs. Also offers training to community partners.	The Buddy-to-Buddy program is a peer partnership model that connects volunteer veteran mentors with service members to help them address various issues and link with community resources.
Steven A. Cohen Military Family Clinic New York University Langone Medical Center	New York University, New York, N.Y.	Clinicians work directly with the Manhattan office of the U.S. Department of Veterans Affairs (VA) and other community partners to offer warm hand-offs, referrals, and clinical services in specialty areas, such as alcohol and substance abuse and grief and loss.	Dual-diagnosis program for veterans, service members, and their family members with addiction and co-occurring mental health issues.

offerings in terms of number of sessions offered and number of individuals trained. WBV outreach and dissemination activities have reached large numbers of individuals, informed them about mental health, and encouraged them to seek mental health care if they need it. Since WBV began, grantees have offered a total of 564 training sessions, attended by 28,736 learners. About half of these sessions train health care providers. Other sessions aim to educate service members and veterans, students, community members, families, friends, and legal professionals serving military populations. Grantees have also leveraged their own expertise in evidence-based treatments (e.g., Prolonged Exposure therapy from Emory University, Cognitive Processing Therapy from Duke, FOCUS from NFRC and Road Home) to increase the number of mental health providers who are trained to deliver these treatments.

Service delivery activities are beginning to have WBV's desired effect. For example, at the end of Phase II, the Duke University Veteran Culture and Clinical Competencies program reported that providers from the Center for Child and Family Health who had completed their cognitive processing therapy training delivered services to veterans and their family members. Future tracking of such effects as these will be valuable in assessing WBV efforts to expand the mental health provider pool.

Raising awareness and promoting help-seeking. Throughout Phase II, grantees conducted outreach and dissemination aimed at increasing awareness about mental health issues and services and encouraging those with mental health needs to seek help. To promote services, grantees participated in community events; organized activities for veterans, service members, and their families; met with key stakeholders; and sent information about programs to targeted audiences. Grantees recognized the importance of communicating with veterans and their families about mental health needs and about the availability of programs. Some WBV sites also partnered with other organizations to disseminate information and recruit individuals into trainings and clinical services. Programs varied in how much they invested in these activities; some leveraged media and local celebrities to help. Many programs also hired veterans as peer outreach specialists, who helped engage other veterans and also offered peer support during service delivery.

Creating referral networks: mental health safety nets. WBV has functioned as a safety net, helping ensure that service members, veterans, and families receive the appropriate mental health care. WBV can fill gaps in coverage by serving veterans, service members, and family members who may be ineligible or unwilling to seek care at VHA, MHS, or private/community health care systems or have not sought care because of financial constraints. WBV can also refer eligible patients to VHA, MHS, and private/community health care programs for long-term or more-intensive care, as needed. In this way, WBV's partnerships and referrals can improve individuals' access to appropriate mental health care from the most appropriate system. In addition, WBV's efforts to raise awareness about mental health and reduce stigma associated with treatment-seeking aim to encourage service members, veterans, and families to understand their mental health options and pursue treatment as needed.

Conclusion

The WBV initiative has enhanced system capacity by providing mental health services for service members, veterans, and their families—including specialized services for specific populations, such as female veterans, service members and veterans with TBI, military and veteran families, service members and veterans with substance abuse issues, and service members and veterans who have experienced military sexual trauma. The initiative also has enhanced capacity by offering training in treatment delivery and cultural competency to thousands of community mental health providers.

In sum, WBV has made strides in assisting service members, veterans, and families and in facilitating collaboration among systems of care in local communities. However, strategic efforts are needed to promote sustainability and address emerging challenges faced by MHS, VHA, and private systems of care.

As public and philanthropic support shifts and resources continue to decline following the drawdown of U.S. forces deployed overseas, WBV grantees and other programs must continue adapting to sustain their mental health service offerings and meet the demand for care. Negotiating third-party payment and expanding collaborative networks may help private mental health care programs, such as WBV, continue to build capacity and have a positive effect going forward.

Efforts must also continue to build on positive changes in MHS, VHA, and community care. Improved use of telemedicine, information technology, and public-private partnerships are promising approaches for bolstering mental health access and quality. While there is no simple, unitary solution for improving the mental health systems for care for service members, veterans, and their families, the combination of these policies and programs will help overcome access and quality challenges within and across the three main systems of care.

Acknowledgments

We wish to thank several individuals for their support of this study. First, we are grateful to Anna LauBach and Donald Cooke from the McCormick Foundation and Tom Brasuell from Major League Baseball for their guidance and collaboration in our performance monitoring efforts. We thank the funded sites within the WBV initiative for their willingness to share information, report data, and host the RAND team during site visits. The sites offered valuable insights from their thoughtful and candid discussions about their goals, processes, challenges, and successes over the course of the project. We are also grateful to the members of the WBV Steering Committee who provided constructive direction on the vision for the initiative.

We acknowledge the support of current and former RAND colleagues Laurie Martin, Racine Harris, Kendra Wilsher, and Clara Aranibar, all of whom helped on this project in prior years. We thank Lisa Jaycox and Kim Hepner for reviewing earlier drafts and providing constructive comments. We also thank our peer reviewers, Rajeev Ramchand and Heather Kelly, for their feedback, which helped to strengthen this report.

Abbreviations

CHAMPVA	Civilian Health and Medical Program of the Department of Veterans Affairs
CPI	continuous performance improvement
CQI	continuous quality improvement
CVN	Cohen Veteran Network
DoD	Department of Defense
EBT	evidence-based treatment
EHR	electronic health record
EVP	Emory's Veterans Program
FOCUS	Families OverComing Under Stress
FY	fiscal year
GAO	U.S. Government Accountability Office
ICARE	integrity, commitment, advocacy, respect, and excellence
HMO	health maintenance organization
IOM	Institute of Medicine, also now called National Academy of Medicine
IT	information technology
MFC	Military Family Clinic
MHS	Military Health System
MLB	Major League Baseball
M-SPAN	Military Support Programs and Networks
MST	military sexual trauma
NFRC	Nathanson Family Resilience Center
NYU	New York University
OEF	Operation Enduring Freedom
OIF	Operation Iraqi Freedom

OND	Operation New Dawn
PC3	Patient-Centered Community Care
PE	Prolonged Exposure
PTSD	posttraumatic stress disorder
SBHP	Star Behavioral Health Providers
TBI	traumatic brain injury
UCLA	University of California, Los Angeles
V3C	Veteran Culture and Clinical Competencies
VA	U.S. Department of Veterans Affairs
VHA	Veterans Health Administration
VISN and MIRECC	South Central Veterans Integrated Service Network 16, Mental Illness Research, Education, and Clinical Center Consumer Guide Workgroup, Sullivan, G., Arlinghaus, K., Edlund, C., & Kauth, M.
WBV	Welcome Back Veterans
WCN	Warrior Care Network
WWP	Wounded Warrior Project

CHAPTER ONE

Introduction

> We have an obligation to evaluate our progress and continue to build an integrated network of support capable of providing effective mental health services for veterans, service members, and their families. Our public health approach must encompass the practices of disease prevention and the promotion of good health for all military populations throughout their lifespans, both within the health care systems of the Departments of Defense and Veterans Affairs and in local communities.
>
> —President Barack Obama (2012)

In the United States, there are an estimated 21 million veterans, 2.2 million service members, and 3.1 million immediate military family members (Substance Abuse and Mental Health Services Administration, 2014). Given ongoing global threats and military activities, the stress of more than a decade of war, and long-standing issues with underutilization of mental health care, projections suggest that mental health care needs across these populations are likely to continue to increase in the coming years (Hoge et al., 2015). The current need for mental health care among these groups is well documented, and research continues to explore the complexities of these issues. Efforts to understand mental health issues within these populations, implement programs to mitigate their impact, develop and disseminate evidence-based practices for treating mental health conditions, and oversee policies and programs have contributed to improvements in treatment approaches. Despite these efforts and investments, challenges remain in forging sustainable, collaborative systems of care that address mental health issues among service members, veterans, and their families.

Veterans Are at Risk for Mental Health Problems

Roughly 2.8 million individuals have deployed to support the recent conflicts in Afghanistan and Iraq (through Operation Enduring Freedom [OEF], Operation Iraqi Freedom [OIF], and Operation New Dawn [OND]). As these individuals return

1

home and separate from military service, most make a successful transition to civilian life, but others face various behavioral health conditions and adjustment challenges (Koblinsky, Leslie, & Cook, 2014). Different research methods, definitions of illnesses and disorders, and populations result in widely varying estimates of the prevalence of posttraumatic stress disorder (PTSD) and major depressive disorder among veterans (Ramchand et al., 2010; Tanielian, Martin, & Epley, 2014). Estimates of mental disorders among OEF and/or OIF service members and veterans vary from 18.5 percent to 42.5 percent (Milliken, Auchterlonie, & Hoge, 2007; Seal et al., 2007; Tanielian & Jaycox, 2008; Seal et al., 2009; National Council for Behavioral Health, 2012). In addition, studies have found that between 11 percent and 20 percent of veterans who served in OEF or OIF met criteria for PTSD at the time of study (Hoge et al., 2004; Hoge, Auchterlonie, & Milliken, 2006; Vasterling et al., 2006; Hoge et al., 2007; Seal et al., 2007; Tanielian & Jaycox, 2008; Institute of Medicine [IOM], 2012; National Center for PTSD, 2016). Recent estimates of depression among OEF/OIF veterans vary from 10 percent to 15 percent (Hoge et al., 2004; Hoge, Auchterlonie, & Milliken, 2006; Vasterling et al., 2006, Hoge et al., 2007; Seal et al. 2007; Tanielian & Jaycox, 2008; IOM, 2012). If untreated, these mental health issues can negatively affect overall health, work productivity, marriage, family relationships, parenting, and social functioning (Tanielian & Jaycox, 2008). PTSD and depression are also linked with higher rates of substance abuse, homelessness, and suicide (Tanielian & Jaycox, 2008; Substance Abuse and Mental Health Services Administration, 2014; Holliday, Pedersen, & Leventhal, 2016).

In addition to OEF/OIF veterans experiencing mental health issues, veterans of earlier conflicts also have rates of PTSD and depression that exceed their nonveteran counterparts (Watkins et al., 2011; Veterans Health Administration [VHA], 2015). For instance, the projected lifetime prevalence of PTSD among male veterans of the Vietnam War is 30.9 percent (Watkins, et al., 2011). Research has also identified high rates of medical comorbidity among veterans of earlier eras with PTSD and such issues as cardiovascular disease and chronic pain (Schnurr & Green, 2004).

Family Members Also Have Mental Health Needs

Family members of service members and veterans also might face mental health challenges, which could manifest while the service member is still in the military or soon or long after the service member transitions to veteran status. To some extent, the academic research literature is more robust with respect to the challenges among active-duty military families in terms of specific mental health needs than it is for veterans' families. For example, there are reports of the rates of mental health utilization among military spouses and military children. Regular surveys of military spouses are conducted by the U.S. Department of Defense (DoD)—e.g., Status of Forces

Survey, Millennium Cohort Family Study—and by some nonprofit military support organizations—e.g., Blue Star Families. These surveys focus on various issues associated with military life. Similar data on the family members of veterans are sparse. While the Millennium Cohort Study is designed to follow service members and their spouses across their military-to-civilian transition, there are no publications from this effort to date that look specifically at issues for the spouse after military separation. There are only a few public-use data sets (e.g., the National Survey of Drug Use and Health, the Medical Expenditure Panel Survey) available that allow the identification of a veteran's family member and very few representative studies of veterans' family members (spouses and children).

The academic research literature on military and veteran families is often categorized on the extent to which the needs may be associated with characteristics of military life (deployment, frequent moves, risk of injury) or of the veteran's disability status (injured versus not injured). Next, we highlight the documented mental health challenges associated with some of these characteristics, including the impact of deployment and the impact of living with a service member or veteran that has a service-connected health problem.

Impacts of Deployment on Military Families

At the time of their deployment, approximately 60 percent of post-9/11 veterans were married, and 50 percent had children. In 2012, DoD estimated that there were approximately 2 million military dependent children (Koblinsky, Leslie, & Cook, 2014). Military families have faced increased deployment tempo and longer deployments over the past decade (Tanielian, Karney, Chandra, & Meadows, 2014). Many studies have linked deployment to military families' poorer mental health, increased behavioral issues in children, and higher rates of divorce and suicide (Meadows, Tanielian, & Karney, 2016). Deployment- and trauma-related stress may be especially harmful to military wives and children (Substance Abuse and Mental Health Services Administration, 2014). Studies of the effects of deployments indicate that military families go through various emotional phases, including anxiety before deployment, worry during deployment, and difficulty readjusting when the service member returns home (Brown et al., 2015).

A recent RAND study (Meadows, Tanielian, & Karney, 2016) examining the impacts of deployment on military families found that they are resilient and that although families face challenges associated with service members' deployments, family relationships typically restore to prior status when service members return home. However, spouses of service members who deployed more often reported that their children had emotional challenges and problems with their peers than did spouses in matched families that did not experience a deployment during the study (Meadows, Tanielian, & Karney, 2016). Teens were especially affected by deployment, reporting poorer family cohesion and worse relationship quality with the nondeployed parent than those reported by teens in families that did not experience a deployment (Meadows, Tanielian, & Karney, 2016).

Other research has shown that children in military families have higher rates of anxiety and more emotional issues and problems at school than others of the same age (Brown et al., 2015). On top of the regular stresses of growing up, military children may experience additional stresses of frequent moves and new schools and peers, missing their parent while the parent is deployed, and having their parent return with illnesses or injuries. Studies have also indicated higher rates of behavioral disorders among military children with a deployed parent compared to those without a deployed parent (Gorman, Eide, & Hisle-Gorman, 2010). Furthermore, deployment is linked with a number of issues for military families, including adverse health effects, increased stress and mental health issues, economic burdens, and higher rates of family violence (IOM, 2013).

There are a number of ways in which a service member's deployment can affect a spouse's well-being: It can induce stress from the separation or the worry about the service member's well-being; it can create new obligations or roles at home; and it can result in a spouse having to make changes to his or her employment situation. But even if the effect of deployment on a spouse is minimal, readjusting to life as a couple after a deployment can be challenging. In addition, military spouses may experience career frustration that affects their emotional and financial well-being (Runge, Waller, MacKenzie, & McGuire, 2014). These issues contribute to the documented high rates of depression among military spouses (Verdeli et al., 2011).

In addition, interpersonal conflict may be an issue for military families. A study of predeployment and postdeployment health assessments of active and reserve soldiers who deployed to Iraq in the recent conflict found that concerns about interpersonal conflict significantly increased after deployment (from 3.5 percent to 14.0 percent among active duty soldiers and from 4.2 percent to 21.2 percent among reserve component soldiers) (Milliken, Auchterlonie, & Hoge, 2007).

Impact of Living with a Veteran Who Has a Service-Connected Health Problem

Studies have also shown that if a veteran has a service-connected health impairment, including PTSD, there may be effects on the family members as well. For example, several studies have noted increased challenges associated with living with a veteran experiencing PTSD and other behavioral health issues (National Center for PTSD, 2015a). Research has shown that Vietnam veterans with PTSD are at higher risk of perpetrating physical, verbal, and psychological aggression against their partners (Byrne and Riggs, 1996). Moreover, one study found that combat veterans account for 21 percent of spouse or partner abuse in the United States (Prigerson, Maciejewski, & Rosenheck, 2002). Increased prevalence of substance abuse among veterans may also have negative effects on military families (National Center for PTSD, 2015b).

Taking on the caregiving role for a wounded, ill, or injured veteran also contributes to mental health problems among military families. Many veterans with illnesses and injuries depend on informal caregivers, family members, friends, or acquaintances for daily care and support (Ramchand et al., 2014). Family members often prioritize caring for the veteran over their personal needs (National Center for PTSD, 2015a). Our prior research estimated that there are 5.5 million military caregivers in the United States, and the time and effort that they spend providing care and support may contribute to the loss of income, jobs, or health care—as well as having physical and emotional effects (Ramchand et al., 2014). In addition, caregivers of post-9/11 veterans encounter family tension and issues at work at higher rates than their caregiver peers whose care recipients are nonmilitary (Ramchand et al., 2014). Furthermore, military caregivers' duties may also affect family dynamics, such as marital quality and capacity to care for children (Ramchand et al., 2014).

Improving Mental Health Outcomes for Veterans and Their Family Members Is a National Priority

Given the increased stress on service members, veterans, and their families, there have been a number of efforts designed to provide medical and nonmedical support for mental health problems. While there has been an expansion in the services and programs available, research also continues to identify gaps in access and to assess the quality of care.

First, mental health care is vitally important to the lives, overall health, and well-being of service members, veterans, and families. Ensuring service members' mental health has key implications for their capacity to engage in their mission and successfully reintegrate after deployment. Mental health care can help prepare for and ease these transitions and can offer higher quality of life and well-being for service members and families.

Mental health and physical health are inextricably linked (Colton and Manderscheid, 2006). Individuals' mental health issues can have negative effects on treatment processes and outcomes of other medical conditions (American Hospital Association, 2012). Individuals with mental illness are more likely to have unhealthy risk factors, such as smoking and obesity, and, as a result, may have higher chances of stroke and diabetes and other chronic conditions (American Hospital Association, 2012). Likewise, on average, individuals with severe mental illness die 25 years earlier than individuals from the general population (Parks, Svendsen, Singer, Foti, & Mauer, 2006). Poor-quality care or lack of access to care may contribute to such negative health outcomes among individuals with mental illness (American Hospital Association, 2012).

Second, experiencing a mental health problem can have ripple effects on many other dimensions of individuals' lives, and the costs of failing to effectively treat mental health issues are high. Untreated mental and behavioral issues can have major effects on social factors. For instance, having behavioral health conditions is associated with greater likelihood of living in poverty, having a lower socioeconomic status, and attaining lower levels of education (Russell, 2010). PTSD has been linked to reductions in physical health, social functioning, and emotional well-being, as well as physical limitations and unemployment (Zatzick et al., 1997). However, research has also demonstrated that evidence-based treatment (EBT) can facilitate recovery and reduce these consequences.

Employees' mental health status affects rates of illness, on-the-job accidents, and staff turnover (Heal, 2000). Individuals' mental and behavioral health conditions may also interfere with their productivity, increase absenteeism, and potentially lead to lowered income and unemployment (American Hospital Association, 2012). Severe mental illness, such as bipolar disorder or chronic depression, can have an even greater impact on employment. In 2007, the annual income of individuals with severe mental illness was $16,000 less than that of the general population (Hogg Foundation for Mental Health and Methodist Healthcare Ministries, 2011). Every year in the United States, individuals' declines in productivity associated with mental disorders result in roughly 217 million days of work lost or partially lost, which is projected to cost employers $21.7 billion annually (American Hospital Association, 2012).

In addition, if behavioral health issues go untreated, the likelihood of these issues rises, as does the likelihood that individuals will become homeless or be incarcerated (Hogg Foundation for Mental Health and Methodist Healthcare Ministries, 2011). One-third of homeless men are veterans (National Coalition for Homeless Veterans, n.d.). The majority of homeless veterans have mental illness, alcohol and/or substance abuse issues, or co-occurring disorders (National Coalition for Homeless Veterans, n.d.).

There are substantial monetary costs associated with substandard and inaccessible mental health care. In 2008, RAND estimated the societal costs of postdeployment mental health problems, such as PTSD and depression, among service members to be approximately $6.2 billion. The study further documented that if all veterans received high-quality care for these conditions, these costs could be reduced by $1.2 billion. Thus, investing in improved access and high-quality care would not only serve to stem the adverse consequences for individuals and their family members, it would also reduce the two-year economic burden on society.

Over the past decade, there have been a number of efforts to make addressing these issues a national priority. These have included increases to the federal budgets within DoD and the U.S. Department of Veterans Affairs (VA) to attend to these issues (i.e., hiring more providers, investing in research, including the creation of new federally funded clinical and research consortia), the issuing of executive orders by the Obama administration, the establishment of Interagency Task Force on Military and Veteran Mental Health and cross-agency priority goals, and the development of the Joining Forces Initiative. These efforts have served to build federal capabilities to address the mental health needs of service members, veterans, and their families in important ways.

While bolstering the federal resources and capacity to address mental health issues among veterans and their families was critically important, there remained limitations in the ability of the government capacity to serve the population. For instance, restrictions on eligibility for benefits and services for veterans may limit access to mental health care from DoD or the VA. This has been an issue particularly for members of the National Guard or Reserve, who are eligible for TRICARE (the DoD health care program) only while they are activated. Access to the VA is also restricted to those who meet certain eligibility requirements that are based on the nature and length of service. At the same time, many military service members and veterans have faced other barriers to using these federal resources, including structural capacity constraints (provider shortages, clinic hours) that have limited availability of services. Some service members and veterans also expressed concerns about confidentiality and fear of career repercussions for seeking care. Thus, many service members, veterans, and their family members turn to nongovernmental sources of support to meet their needs.

To respond to the new demand for community support from veterans and their families, there has been a concurrent expansion of efforts to increase capacity to support these populations in the nongovernmental sector. One of these efforts is the Welcome Back Veterans (WBV) initiative. Major League Baseball (MLB) and the Robert R. McCormick Foundation launched WBV in 2008 to support organizations that, in turn, provided programs and services to support veterans and their families. Since its founding, WBV has issued grants to academic medical institutions around the nation to create and implement programs and services designed to address the mental health needs of returning veterans and their families.

Organization of This Report

This report offers insights on enhancing mental health care systems for service members, veterans, and families based on research on and analysis of WBV. In Chapter Two, we provide context for how our nation addresses these issues by describing the military and veterans' mental health care systems and highlighting recent innovations and challenges across these systems of care. We review the two major systems of care designed to address the health care needs of service members and veterans—DoD and the VA—and provide a backdrop for how nongovernmental programs add capacity in our national landscape of support for the mental health needs of service members, veterans, and their families. In Chapter Three, we describe the activities of WBV in greater detail, highlighting some of their effects and contributions to the nation's capacity to support service members, veterans, and their families. Chapter Four highlights some remaining challenges for the nongovernmental sector and briefly describes newer initiatives on the horizon. Finally, Chapter Five provides some perspectives and recommendations for how efforts across the government and nongovernment sectors could be better coordinated and integrated to close remaining gaps in access to high-quality mental health care for our nation's service members, veterans, and their families.

CHAPTER TWO

Understanding and Influencing Federal Health Systems of Care for Mental Health

During the last decade, the Military Health System (MHS), the VHA, and nonmilitary community and private-sector systems have added a number of new programs and policies aimed at improving access to and quality of mental health care for service members, veterans, and their families. These efforts include increasing integration and coordination among these historically separate systems of care. A major challenge, however, has been helping service members, veterans, and their families understand their options and navigate the different systems of care. They may not be aware of the various offerings, may feel overwhelmed by available choices, or may not know the most effective option for their particular need. This section offers an overview of DoD, VA, and community, private, or nongovernmental mental health care for service members, veterans, and their families. Later in the chapter, we describe the limitations of these systems of care, major shifts and changes in the capacity of these sectors to provide access to high-quality mental health care, and policy changes over the past decade that affect these systems.

The Current Systems of Care

There are three main systems of care in which service members, veterans, and their families may seek mental health care: MHS, VHA, and the community, private, or nongovernmental health care sector. The MHS and VHA provide both direct care (i.e., through military treatment facilities and VHA medical centers, respectively) and purchased care (i.e., paid for by the MHS or VHA but delivered by nonmilitary providers). These three sectors serve overlapping populations of military personnel, veterans, and their families, many of whom may be eligible for care in more than one system. Complicating navigation of the systems of care is the range of eligibility requirements and health care options for these patients. For example, the majority of veterans are also covered by Medicare, Medicaid, or private health insurance plans, and many DoD beneficiaries also have other forms of health coverage (Merlis, 2012). While most family members are not eligible for direct VA care, some family members are eligible

Table 2.1
Overview of Federal Care Options for Military Service Members and Veterans

Program	Eligibility	Design	Cost Sharing
TRICARE Prime	• Active duty military and some Reservists and their families • Retirees (generally with 20+ years of service) and their dependents; medical retirees	• HMO with primary care from military facilities or specialty care from military or contracted civilian providers • HMO with primary care from military facilities or contracted providers	• No enrollment fee or copayments for in-network care; deductibles and coinsurance for out-of-network care
TRICARE Standard	• MHS beneficiaries other than active duty personnel	• Fee-for-service with care from military facilities or civilian providers; reduced cost-sharing when participants use TRICARE Extra contacted providers	• No enrollment fee; deductible, 20–25 percent coinsurance and potential provider balance-billing
TRICARE Extra	• Preferred provider organization–like option for all TRICARE Standard participants	• Same as TRICARE Standard	• Same as TRICARE Standard except lower coinsurance and no balance-billing for in network providers
TRICARE for Life	• Medicare-enrolled retirees for 20+ years of service and dependents	• Medicare wraparound	• Services covered by TRICARE but not by Medicare are subject to deductible and coinsurance
Veteran Health Care	• Honorably discharged veterans with 24+ months of active service and some Reservists/National Guard members called up on federal orders • Priority enrollment for low-income recipients and those with service-connected disabilities • Some mental health services available to those with other than honorable discharges • Individuals serving after 9/11 can access VHA without enrolling for up to five years after discharge	• Inpatient and outpatient care provided by VHA facilities or purchased from community providers, prescription drugs, and some long-term care	• Cost-sharing for treatment of non–service-connected conditions for some priority groups of veterans

Reservists serving on active duty are recognized as having veteran status and may be eligible for VA benefits, and National Guard members may also be eligible if they are activated in combat or domestic emergency (VA, n.d.). However, Reservists and National Guard members have limited eligibility for VA health care when they are not on full-time activation for federal service.

VA health care is allocated based on the availability of resources (Panangala, 2016). Thus, VA health care eligibility is dependent on the agency's budget. VA uses a "priority group" system to determine eligibility and resource allocation for groups of veterans. The priority group system is determined based on veterans' service-connected disabilities, income, service during a conflict, commendations, and other factors. Enrollees never pay for care on service-connected conditions, and copayments for non–service-connected conditions vary based on their priority group.

Special exceptions have been made to increase access to VA health care for veterans who have recently returned from combat. Within five years of returning from combat, veterans are eligible to enroll in VA health care without needing to prove that their illness or injury is service-connected or meet an income requirement (Panangala, 2016). Once veterans enroll in VA care under the extended eligibility authority, they may continue receiving health care beyond the five-year eligibility period (Panangala, 2016).

In mid-2017, the VA Secretary announced plans to open up some mental health services for veterans with other than honorable discharges. This policy change was largely motivated by concerns over the increased rate of suicide among veterans with discharge statuses that were other than honorable. On July 5, 2017, these veterans became eligible for VA emergency mental health services. As of this writing, it is not known how this policy change will affect demand and utilization for these services or how the longer-term mental health needs of this population will be met by the VA health care system.

Veteran Health Administration Mission and Mental Health Care

VHA's mission is to "Honor America's Veterans by providing exceptional health care that improves their health and well-being" (VHA, 2017). VHA is the largest integrated health care organization in the United States, with approximately 150 medical centers, more than 800 community-based outpatient clinics (CBOCs), 135 community living centers, 278 Vet Centers, and 48 domiciliaries (residential treatment programs) (VHA, 2017). In 2015, approximately 6.7 million veterans used VHA health care, out of approximately 9 million VHA-enrolled veterans (VA, 2017) (in a total population of more than 21 million veterans) (Bagalman, 2014).

In 2015, VHA also provided specialized mental health treatment to more than 1.4 million veterans (VA, 2017). VHA offers evidence-based outpatient and inpatient mental health direct care for a wide range of issues, including depression, anxiety, PTSD, substance abuse, bipolar disorder, and schizophrenia (South Central Veterans Integrated Service Network 16, Mental Illness Research, Education, and Clinical Center Consumer Guide Workgroup, Sullivan, G., Arlinghaus, K., Edlund, C., & Kauth, M. [VISN and MIRECC], 2011). VHA offers mental health care at medical centers, CBOCs (either in-person or via telehealth), and domiciliaries. In addition, Vet Centers specialize in readjustment counseling and MST counseling and offer services at no cost for family members dealing with military-related issues, including bereavement (VISN and MIRECC, 2011). In addition, VHA offers supported work settings and residential care for veterans who need mental health and rehabilitative care (VISN and MIRECC, 2011).

VHA also provides specialized and coordinated mental health care. VHA Suicide Prevention Coordinators collaborate with mental health care teams and offer specialized support for veterans at high risk for suicide (VISN and MIRECC, 2011). The Veterans Crisis Line is a toll-free, confidential hotline, online chat, and text service that connects qualified VHA responders with veterans in crisis and their families and friends 24 hours a day, seven days a week. In addition, any veteran who experienced MST is eligible for VHA counseling, including specialized inpatient, outpatient, and residential programs (VISN and MIRECC, 2011). VHA also offers a range of services for veterans who are homeless, older (with nursing home needs), or involved with the criminal justice system who may also need mental health care (VISN and MIRECC, 2011).

In addition to providing direct treatment and services, VHA purchases care for veterans from the community or private sector through a variety of programs. The amount of purchased care has grown in recent years and may expand further as a result of the Veterans Choice Act, through which VHA may purchase care from private providers for veterans who live more than 40 miles from the nearest VHA facility or who are unable to get a needed health care appointment within 30 days.

Community-Based or Private-Sector Provided Care

As discussed earlier, both MHS and VHA purchase care from the community or private sector as needed and appropriate to meet the needs of their covered populations. In addition, service members, veterans, and their family members may be eligible for health care in the community or private sector through a wide array of options based on their own individual circumstances. These could include private health insurance provided by an employer or purchased independently, Medicare or Medicaid, Indian Health Service, federally qualified health centers, and student health centers, as well as care provided by or coordinated through nonprofit organizations. Some individuals may be eligible for care in multiple systems, either sequentially or simultaneously. For example, a member of the Reserve component is automatically enrolled in TRICARE Prime when serving on active duty for more than 30 days but may return to using VHA or employer-sponsored health care when not on active duty status. Others may get prescription medication through VHA while concurrently getting mental health counseling through a nonprofit service provider. For those with multiple options for care, the choice of which system to access for what type of care may be based on personal preferences, geographic proximity, wait times, cost, perceptions of confidentiality and quality, or other factors.

Community and Private-Sector Mission and Mental Health Care

In caring for service members, veterans, and their families, the community and private sector help support the missions of MHS and VHA. Community and private-sector providers have overlapping but distinct roles in serving the mental health care needs of military and veteran populations. Community providers and programs that participate in MHS and VHA purchased care programs have a direct role in supporting surge capacity needs for DoD and the VA. Beyond serving military and veteran populations, community providers aim to fulfill the broader mission of meeting the diverse health care needs of the local population.

On the other hand, while some privately funded providers and centers aim to meet diverse local health care needs, others specifically seek to fill the gaps in mental health care for service members, veterans, and their families and create new capacity to provide mental health care for them in a number of ways. By offering accessible, high-quality care, privately funded centers and programs increase the availability of providers and appointments, which may reduce wait times and encourage treatment-seeking among military and veterans' populations. Some new centers and programs offer mental health care for veterans and their families who may not be eligible for VA care, including those with dishonorable discharges. For these individuals, in particular, private providers help increase access to mental health care. Many privately funded centers offer free mental health care services, eliminating financial barriers to care for some service members, veterans, and their families. At the same time, some privately funded centers and programs aim to complement the VHA by offering services that are not typically available there, including child mental health services, nontraditional therapies (e.g., equine therapy, hyperbaric oxygen therapy, or wraparound case management services).

Ultimately, although the community's and private sector's purviews and processes differ, both groups contribute meaningfully to improving the accessibility of quality care for military and veteran populations across the United States.

Recent Delivery Innovations in Expanding Capacity to High-Quality Mental Health Care

MHS, VHA, and community and private providers have sought to innovate with new technical systems and integrated health care settings to improve access and quality of mental health care. There have been two major system-level shifts in recent years: tele–mental health and mental health in primary care. These innovations seek to improve the structural capacity of MHS and VHA to meet the high demand for mental health care. The approaches also aim to reduce barriers to care posed by provider shortages, geographic distance, and stigma, which are discussed in greater detail later in this chapter.

Tele–Mental Health

With the increasing availability and sophistication of video and other technology applications, many health care providers have started using telehealth approaches to extend the reach of their services. For some, this may be the simple use of the telephone to provide consultations to patients and other providers, or it might be the more sophisticated use of web-based platforms to share images and videos to provide care virtually. Over the past decade, the VHA has used telehealth to expand access to mental health care for veterans, particularly for those veterans who may live too far away to easily reach a facility with specialty mental health care services. VHA's tele–mental health care includes the use of web-based communication platforms for delivering services to veterans in venues not colocated with the primary therapist. In these instances, a VA mental health professional interacts with a patient who may be sitting in a different community-based outpatient setting or a Vet Center. The use of these approaches has begun to take effect: Approximately 100,000 veterans living in remote communities have received mental health care through that medium (Office of Rural Health, 2015). As shown in Figure 2.1, VHA spending on telehealth has risen substantially in recent years. The requested 2017 budget for telehealth is $1.2 billion, up by 5.1 per-

Figure 2.1
VHA Spending on Telehealth, FYs 2013–2017

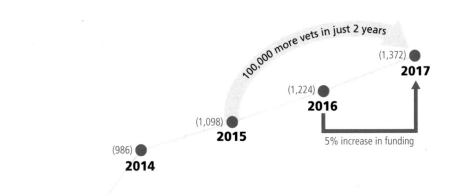

SOURCES: VA, 2007–2011.
NOTE: FY 2016 is enacted funding; FY 2017 is requested funding.
RAND RR2030-2.1

cent from the 2016 level (VA, 2017). In 2015, VHA provided telehealth services to more than 677,000 veterans and plans to provide telehealth services to approximately 762,000 veterans in 2017 (VA, 2017).

Beyond formal telehealth services, VA's National Center for PTSD has partnered with DoD's National Center for Telehealth and Technology to develop a suite of free, publicly available mobile applications, including both self-help apps (e.g., PTSD Coach, Mindfulness Coach) and treatment companion apps for those working with a therapist on cognitive processing or Prolonged Exposure [PE] therapy (National Center for PTSD, 2017a). These are intended to be tools for self-management that can supplement and complement provider-based care. Studies have indicated that PTSD Coach is well-received by veterans (Gordon, S., 2016). Aimed at teaching users to manage PTSD symptoms, the app offers information about PTSD and treatment, as well as tools for screening and tracking symptoms; it has been downloaded more than 100,000 times from 74 countries around the world (National Center for PTSD, 2017b). Early evaluation results indicate that users found PTSD Coach to be helpful in reducing their symptoms (Kuhn et al., 2014).

In addition to these specific mental health treatment apps, other advancements in technology may influence how veterans can access mental health care services. For example, the VHA has introduced a new scheduling application that is intended to help make scheduling and managing appointments easier. The VA Secretary also recently announced plans to adopt the DoD's electronic medical record system, thereby making the transfer and sharing of medical records much more seamless and enabling greater continuity of care for service members and veterans with mental health problems. While this change has yet to be implemented, this announcement followed nearly two decades of discussions about the integration of electronic medical records for these two large health systems.

Providing Mental Health Services in Primary Care

Mental health care has been integrated into primary care in all three systems in order to reduce mental health treatment stigma and to increase patient satisfaction, access to care, and the effectiveness of evidence-based care. MHS has implemented this integration across all installations and clinics as part of its patient-centered medical home (PCMH) model, and some of the individual service branches have gone even further, embedding behavioral health providers within operational units (Embrey, 2009; Julian, 2013). VHA's conceptualization of PCMHs, referred to as patient-aligned care teams (Patient Care Services, 2016), seeks to offer patient-driven, personalized care that includes proactive screening and treatment for mental health issues in the primary care setting (Rosland et al., 2013). Within the private sector, larger health care systems have also sought to implement PCMHs and community care organizations to improve the integration of mental health and primary care (Brink, 2014).

However, there are some challenges associated with treating mental health issues in the primary care setting. In short appointments, primary care providers are tasked with diagnosing and treating a number of issues. Identifying and treating both physical ailments and mental health issues can be difficult in the primary care environment. Research has shown that general practitioners often fail to diagnose and treat individuals with mental disorders (Jorm, 2000). More than one-third of patients who seek mental health care are treated through primary care as the only form of health care they use (Russell, 2010). However, primary care doctors recognize the mental health problems of less than one-third (31 percent) of those patients (Ani et al., 2008). Moreover, given concerns about the physician supply shortage, particularly in the primary care workforce, some fear that asking primary care providers to do more in mental health provision will further stretch these personnel (IHS Markit, 2016). This additional tasking should be considered in the development of and planning for primary care capacity, training, and education (Russell, 2010).

In addition to concerns about capacity and timeliness of care, quality of mental health care in the primary care setting has also been a concern. Primary care providers do not always provide evidence-based care for mental health issues (Russell, 2010). For instance, studies have found that primary care providers do not always prescribe the appropriate dosages of antidepressants or schedule the required follow-up visits (Russell, 2010). Furthermore, primary care providers often do not provide referrals for psychotherapy— and when they do, many patients either do not follow up to receive that care or they drop out quickly. This is a significant limitation because certain types of psychotherapy are first-line treatment options for several psychiatric disorders, and many patients prefer psychotherapy (Russell, 2010). To address some of these concerns, VHA and other settings (including MHS) have begun embedding trained mental health professionals (e.g., psychologists, social workers, and psychiatrists) directly into the primary care setting. Placing mental health professionals in primary care is a component of some integrated behavioral health models, but with embedded approaches, there is usually less focus on training the primary care professional to manage mental health problems. Rather, primary care providers refer patients to a mental health provider in the same physical setting and do not deliver the psychiatric services themselves.

Incorporating Peer-Specialists into Health Care Settings

In the veteran and military support community, peer support is a common phenomenon. Many military and veteran support organizations provide veterans with an opportunity to connect with each other, share their experiences, and provide social support. Some organizations specifically use peers in official roles to help navigate benefits and systems (such as an ombudsman or peer navigator). The evidence on whether peers improve outcomes for other veterans is scant, and the literature on the empirical support for involving peers in health-related interventions is mixed, largely based on the role and function of the peer (Ramchand et al., 2017). Over the past several years, the

VA and nongovernmental sources of mental health services have worked to incorporate peers into their continuum of mental health services. Recognizing the strong desire and interest that veterans have in connecting with other veterans, these peer-specialists have been incorporated into settings as gatekeepers—facilitating connections and access to services as mentors and care coaches to augment and support treatment retention. In 2016, the Obama administration tasked VA and DoD with integrating peer-specialists not only into their mental health sites but also into primary care settings. These peer-specialists are specifically trained to help coordinate care and facilitate the health and well-being of veterans.

Expanding Access to Community Sources of Care

Both DoD and VHA have sought to expand access to mental health services by bolstering their networks of community-based providers. For the VA, these changes were particularly accelerated after the passage of the VA Choice Act in 2014. This legislation mandated that the VA allow VHA enrollees to seek care in the community if they lived more than 40 miles from a VA facility or if their wait for care was more than 30 days. After the initial implementation of the VA Choice Program, VA requested further revisions to the eligibility criteria, aiming to eliminate the strict criteria for distance and time, instead desiring a more clinically based approach to determining when community care would be authorized.

DoD also sought to increase the number of mental health providers who would accept TRICARE by calling on its managed care support contractors to increase network enrollment of licensed mental health professionals. Historically, concerns over TRICARE reimbursement rates limited network expansion, and the new effort is no exception; concerns about reimbursement rates continue. Paradoxically, rather than using reimbursement increases to entice more providers into the network, some managed care contractors have recently proposed reductions in reimbursement rates for mental health care within TRICARE, which has intensified concerns among mental health providers about network participation.

Remaining Concerns and Challenges

While MHS, VHA, and community/private systems are innovating to improve their treatment and services, issues with mental health care access and quality persist. Shortages of trained, culturally competent clinicians; driving distance; and perceptions about the consequences of seeking care may make present obstacles for veterans, service members, and family members in accessing mental health care. We discuss these issues briefly.

Shortage of Behavioral Health Providers

Nationwide, there is a shortage of mental health providers, which is worsening at a time when individuals are gaining support—logistically, emotionally, and financially—to seek treatment. Multiple efforts have been put in place to increase recognition of mental health issues and encourage care-seeking among service members and veterans; however, continued concern about the availability of providers remains. As of September 8, 2016, mental health professionals were meeting only about 48 percent of the need for care (Henry J. Kaiser Family Foundation, 2016).

This shortage affects all three systems of care, affecting appointment availability and consistency, as well as quality of care. To address issues with provider shortages, MHS and VHA have not only integrated mental health in primary care and expanded the use of tele–mental health options, they also have hired more providers. To meet increased demand (and respond to congressional requirements), both departments have implemented significant hiring and retention initiatives. MHS has taken steps to make hiring civilian mental health providers easier (Under Secretary of Defense for Personnel and Readiness, 2015) and sought to attract mental health providers by using direct-hire authority and compensation incentives (Under Secretary of Defense for Personnel and Readiness, 2015), thus boosting recruitment and hiring for many clinical positions (Under Secretary of Defense for Personnel and Readiness, 2015). This was coupled with a concerted effort to expand the number of mental health clinicians in the TRICARE network. In VHA, shortages of providers and other personnel may contribute to reductions in accessibility and quality of care (Hussey et al., 2015). In a recent RAND study of VHA resources and capacity, the most frequently cited workforce shortage was in psychiatry and/or mental health, with roughly one-third of facilities surveyed indicating a shortage (Hussey et al., 2015). VHA also has had physician and specialist shortages, including mental health, in certain geographic areas (Hussey et al., 2015). Although the mental health provider shortage has been recognized, the Government Accountability Office (GAO) found in 2015 that VHA was not strategically recruiting, hiring, and maintaining psychiatrists on staff (GAO, 2015a).

The issue of mental health provider shortages extends beyond VHA. The United States has a national shortage of mental health care providers. There are fewer health care providers working in rural areas in the United States, and about 80 percent of rural areas are classified as medically underserved (Brown et al., 2015). Recent research has confirmed that health professional shortages overlap with many military-specific provider shortage areas, including psychiatrists, psychologists, and therapists (Brown et al., 2015). Thus, military, veteran, and civilian systems of care are competing for the same limited pool of mental health care providers.

In 2012, President Obama issued an executive order to task VHA with hiring 1,600 mental health professionals and 800 peer-to-peer counselors to help meet the demand for care (Obama, 2012), which VHA fulfilled in 2013 (VA, 2013). In 2015, VHA increased its mental health workforce with the recruitment and hiring of

2,467 mental health providers for vacant positions, 1,720 mental health clinicians for newly created positions, and more than 960 peer-specialists and peer support apprentices (National Center for PTSD, 2015a).

Despite this expansion, GAO found that VHA continues to struggle to manage mental health care appointments; in some cases, veterans have waited nine months for evaluations (GAO, 2015a). GAO noted that VHA's unclear policies on wait times and mismanaged and unreliable data prevent the organization from effectively overseeing effective scheduling, and it recommended that VHA provide better guidance on various policies on veterans' access to care, definitions used to calculate wait times, and management of open appointments (GAO, 2015a).

While MHS and VHA have made significant investments in expanding its mental health workforce, it should be noted that nonmilitary care systems continue to face difficulties in providing mental health care as well. In the United States, 42.5 million adults have a mental illness, and 41 percent of them report seeking treatment (Radnofsky, 2015). As the nationwide shortage of providers continues, incentivizing mental health providers to work for MHS or VHA may compromise access and quality of care offered at community health organizations, which may already be understaffed (Gugliotta, 2013). Long-term solutions must focus on increasing the number of qualified mental health providers overall.

Cultural Competence of Providers

The increased emphasis on community-based care for service members, veterans, and their families has led to greater consideration of how best to care for them outside MHS and VHA settings. One important concern is whether providers in the private sector have the appropriate competencies to serve veterans and their families. The concept of military cultural competence has been used to refer to a provider's knowledge, skills, and abilities to deliver sensitive care to military- and veteran-affiliated patients. A 2014 RAND study found that mental health providers' comfort when treating service members, veterans, and their families varies greatly (Tanielian et al., 2014). The researchers found that, among those surveyed, mental health providers' knowledge of military and veteran culture was generally poor (Tanielian et al., 2014). Those mental health providers who demonstrated higher levels of military cultural competence were more likely to work in a DoD or VHA setting or accept TRICARE; providers without such affiliations may have lower levels of military cultural competence (Tanielian et al., 2014).

To address the level of sensitivity in the private sector, training courses in military cultural competency have mushroomed over the last several years, with a range of courses varying in intensity from short webinars to longer in-person sessions. Among them is the VHA Community Provider Toolkit, an online forum that community providers can use to inform the mental health care services they provide to veterans; it includes information on mental health conditions, connecting with VA, and military culture (VA Mental Health, n.d.). The site also offers information on how to screen patients for military affiliation and/or experience, as well as online military cultural competency training and mini-clinics, which are lessons on treating veterans with various mental health conditions (VA Mental Health, n.d.).

Geographic Access to Mental Health Care

Approximately 3,000 service members and 1 million dependents have a commute of 30 minutes or more to access behavioral health care, and beneficiaries who live in remote locations make 20 percent fewer visits to behavioral health providers (Brown et al., 2015), which means they may not be getting the care they need. Policymakers and researchers have identified tele–mental health and collaborative care as two approaches for overcoming challenges associated with service members and their families living in remote areas (Brown et al., 2015). Accordingly, MHS has taken steps to expand access to mental health services for service members and eligible family members who live in remote locations (Under Secretary of Defense for Personnel and Readiness, 2015). For example, in 2008, the Defense Centers of Excellence for Psychological Health and Traumatic Brain Injury developed the Telehealth and Technology Center, which aims to advance innovation in integrating technology in mental health care for service members, veterans, and family members (Under Secretary of Defense for Personnel and Readiness, 2015).

Similarly, health care provider and specialist shortages, appointment wait times, distance to medical facilities, and broadband coverage (for tele–mental health services) can be barriers to care for the approximately 5.3 million veterans living in remote areas (Office of Rural Health, 2014). With the aim of improving health care and services for this growing population, VHA established the Office of Rural Health in December 2006 (Watkins et al., 2011). VA has sought to enhance rural veterans' access to quality care for veterans through partnerships with other VA program offices, federal and state organizations, and rural communities (Office of Rural Health, 2014) and by leveraging technology, investing in research, training community providers in military cultural competence, and implementing innovative recruitment strategies (Watkins et al., 2011). Training efforts aimed at rural and remote communities are building capacity. Clergy members living in remote locales have been trained to better recognize PTSD among returning service members and veterans, and 97 mental health student trainees completed clinical rotations at rural VA facilities (Office of Rural Health, 2015).

Attitudes and Perceptions of Care

Perceptions of the consequences of care (often referred to as stigma) can be a barrier to seeking mental health treatment and are particularly salient in the military. Frequently, commanders are considered part of the care team, and although they are not health providers, they may have access to medical records (Neuhauser, 2010). Lack of confidentiality about mental health and mental health care is associated with stigma and fear of negative career repercussions within the military. Policy language excluding service members with mental health disorders from career opportunities may prevent some service members from seeking care (Acosta et al., 2014; Acosta et al., 2016). Some have indicated that they prefer community care because it offers increased likelihood of confidentiality and available appointments outside work hours (Tanielian et al., 2016). Because of the potential barriers to care associated with lack of confidentiality, studies have recommended that the role of commanders in mental health service delivery be reconsidered (Engel, 2014). Despite these recommendations, commanders still have access to service members' health information under current policy.

Service members' attitudes may also be driven by personal perceptions and experiences. Potential consequences associated with treatment-seeking can lead service members to hide mental illness from family, friends, and colleagues for fear of personal embarrassment, disappointing comrades, losing the opportunity for career advancement, and dishonorable discharge (American Psychological Association, n.d.). Research on stigma suggests both strengths and weaknesses in policy and institutional culture within DoD. On the one hand, research suggests that DoD efforts to reduce stigma associated with mental health treatment–seeking reflect best practices and may contribute to reduced self-reported stigma among service members (Acosta et al., 2016). On the other, stigma continues to be a barrier to mental health treatment for some service members and veterans, and stakeholders have recommended a range of policy solutions, including collaborative care (incorporating behavioral health into primary care settings) and improved confidentiality of mental health care.

DoD has made efforts to encourage service members to seek mental health care if they feel they need it. Under recently changed security clearance procedures, service members do not need to disclose treatment for combat-related issues or marital counseling. In addition, some communications about military mental health policies seek to assure service members that getting help will not impact their careers, and many leaders have come forward to disclose their own help-seeking behavior. Service members are also warned that if their commanding officer observes their symptoms, they may face duty limitations or separations if they do not seek the mental health care they need (National Alliance on Mental Illness, n.d.).

These concerns about career repercussions, combined with other attitudes and perceptions about mental health, are a problem in the VHA and in private and community systems of care as well. These concerns are often bundled under the label of stigma, which is also a documented problem in the civilian community, both in the United States and abroad (Russell, 2010). Over the past decade, several policy and program solutions have been promulgated to reduce stigma associated with mental health treatment-seeking. Providing mental health care in such integrated settings as primary care might minimize stigma and improve health outcomes (Collins, Hewson, Munger, & Wade, 2010). Because perceptions of mental health disorders and treatment can hamper help-seeking (Jorm, 2000), these attitudes have been the target of dissemination and education policies and programs. To reduce stigma, efforts are also under way to improve mental health literacy and public knowledge and opinions about mental disorders (Collins, Hewson, Munger, & Wade, 2010).

Quality of Care

The best mental health outcomes are associated with accessible, high-quality care. The IOM defines quality in health care as "the degree to which health care services for individuals and populations increase the likelihood of desired health outcomes and are consistent with current professional knowledge" (Plsek, 2001).

Quality of mental health care is determined based on a number of performance dimensions and considerations. Consideration of patient preferences and values and use of evidence-based practices are two key components of quality care (IOM, 2006). Another important aspect of quality-of-care is integration of emerging research and technologies for improving mental health treatment practices (IOM, 2006). Other characteristics of quality care include cultural competence of providers; individualization; respect; privacy; professionalism; a holistic approach to health; and provision of care that is inclusive of family, friends, and caregivers.

The definition of quality may also vary based on stakeholder perspective. For example, a patient's definition of quality mental health care may concentrate on symptom reduction; a family member's definition might include his or her role and integration in care; a provider may emphasize the standard of treatment offered; and a policymaker may consider quality of mental health as it applies to larger populations of people and patients (Funk, Lund, Freeman, & Drew, 2009). Health care providers should consider these various perspectives when aiming to implement high-quality mental health care or programs to monitor the delivery of high-quality care. Use of quality measures, information technology (IT) systems, and evidence-based practices can also improve processes and outcomes in mental health care (Kilbourne, Keyser, & Pincus, 2010).

In addition to challenges with access to mental health care, problems with inconsistent quality of care persist. Only about half of returning service members who need mental health treatment seek care, and just over half of those who seek treatment receive care that is at least minimally adequate (Tanielian and Jaycox, 2008). PTSD and major depression are likely to continue to be highly prevalent among service members and veterans unless policy and program changes substantially enhance quality of care for service members, veterans, and their families (Tanielian and Jaycox, 2008).

An IOM 2001 report highlighted the "quality chasm" between the highest-quality, evidence-based health care practices and the much poorer quality of care that most Americans receive (Plsek, 2001). Since then, the United States has undertaken a number of efforts to improve the quality of health care, and the VA and DoD have added personnel and resources to mental health clinics, tested new approaches through various pilot programs, and adjusted policies to improve the quality of mental health care. In addition, to improve quality of mental health care for service members, veterans, and their families, systems of care have sought to enhance performance management, expand implementation of evidence-based practices, and develop monitoring and oversight of processes and patient outcomes.

While progress has been made, more is needed. EBTs for mental health needs are not available in all health care settings (Tanielian and Jaycox, 2008). Although VHA has a number of quality measures and monitoring systems in place, DoD and civilian systems of care do not have robust performance-monitoring tools for quality improvement of mental health care (Burnam, Meredith, Tanielian, & Jaycox, 2009; Hepner et al., 2016; Hepner, Ferris, et al., 2017; Hepner, Sloss, et al., 2017). In addition, a recent RAND study on VA capacity found that, although VA health care quality fared well on many measures and domains compared with non-VA providers, quality performance was inconsistent across VA facilities, and quality improvement is needed in many areas (Hussey et al., 2015). Research has also pointed to insufficient data collection to track quality and hold programs accountable for mental health care for service members, veterans, and their families (Watkins et al., 2011). Furthermore, better evaluation of community mental health providers is needed to assess their capacity to serve veterans, service members, and families as well as the standard of treatment and services they deliver (Tanielian, Farris, et al., 2014).

Summary

VHA, MHS, and private and community providers offer a number of pathways to mental health care for service members, veterans, and their families, some of which may be used sequentially or concurrently as circumstances change. VHA, MHS, and private and community providers have sought to improve access to quality care through collaborative care models and tele–mental health. These solutions are promising, but questions remain regarding implementation, including whether providers are sufficiently competent and comfortable treating service members' and veterans' mental health conditions in the primary care setting and with tele–mental health. In addition, MHS, VHA, and private and community providers face a number of challenges associated with the national shortage of behavioral health providers, inadequate cultural competence of providers, geographic access to mental health care, attitudes and perceptions of mental health care, and variation in quality of care.

To address these issues, privately funded centers and programs have sought to fill gaps in treatment and services and expand community capacity to provide mental health care to service members, veterans, and families. The next chapter describes the role of WBV, one such effort from the private sector.

CHAPTER THREE

Role of WBV Initiative in Strengthening Systems and Extending Community Capacity

Given the various challenges that exist in MHS, VHA, and community systems of mental health care, various efforts have emerged to fill gaps in care and enhance capacity of these systems. Launched in 2008, WBV was designed to support veterans returning from Iraq and Afghanistan and their families as veterans reintegrated into their home communities. Over time and through more-selective grantmaking by the Robert R. McCormick Foundation, WBV has been primarily focused on bolstering the mental health of veterans and their families by reducing barriers to treatment; improving access through direct services offered; and enhancing skills, knowledge, and abilities of the mental health providers across the United States. As programs within the initiative built out their efforts, they initiated a series of innovative approaches to provider training, peer support services, and tele–mental health in an effort to disseminate more and more-effective mental health care practices into a wider range of health care settings. As an initiative, WBV partners prioritized the cultivation of public-private partnerships to facilitate greater coordination and collaboration with MHS, VHA, and community mental health systems.

WBV's development, evolution, and experience offer important insights for various military and veterans' mental health care programs as they seek to address enduring challenges and improve collaboration. This chapter provides an overview of WBV's background and initial development, as well as its later evolution. We describe the overall effect of WBV on expanding the provider base and provider competency through training, to raise awareness and promote help-seeking among veterans and their family members through outreach and dissemination activities, and to deliver clinical care services. This chapter also discusses WBV's efforts to enhance system capacity by offering specialized services for female veterans, service members and veterans with traumatic brain injury (TBI), military and veteran families, service members and veterans with substance abuse issues, and service members and veterans who have experienced MST and by establishing referral networks. We also highlight key lessons learned about facilitators of success by summarizing challenges faced, opportunities missed, and solutions implemented.

Background

WBV is currently a network of academic medical centers that conduct research; provide clinical mental health services (evaluation, treatment, and referral) for service members, veterans, and their families; and offer education and training for a range of military- and veteran-affiliated groups, including health care providers, military caregivers, military and veteran families, and service members and veterans. WBV was founded in 2008 through support from the Robert R. McCormick Foundation and MLB Charities (Tanielian, Martin, & Epley, 2014). In collaboration with DoD, VA, other government organizations, private organizations, and nonprofit organizations, WBV aims to meet the postdeployment mental health needs of veterans returning from Iraq and Afghanistan as well as service members and military families (Tanielian, Martin, & Epley, 2014).

WBV has evolved over the years as the Robert R. McCormick Foundation, MLB, and the WBV Steering Committee reviewed performance and focused efforts on areas where grantees can have the greatest effect. Initially, WBV granted approximately $6 million to 37 nonprofit organizations that served various interests, including employment and career development, family support, and treatment for mental health problems (Tanielian, Martin, & Epley, 2014). In 2010, following an in-depth review of grantee experience and progress, along with some internal strategic planning, McCormick and MLB narrowed the focus of WBV to the mental health needs of returning service members, veterans and their families (Tanielian, Martin, & Epley, 2014). To date, WBV has provided more than $30 million to nonprofit organizations and academic medical centers through three rounds of grants (Welcome Back Veterans, 2016). In the following sections, we briefly describe the nature of the post-2010 activities funded within WBV.

Phase I of WBV Grantmaking (2010–2013)

In 2010, McCormick issued an invitation-only request for proposals to eight academic medical institutions for WBV funding that was intended to focus on three objectives:

1. Transform the lives of returning veterans and their families by facilitating ongoing treatment and support for PTSD, depression, suicide prevention, and other mental health concerns.
2. Complement VA, DoD, and community-agency services through the development of public-private partnerships.
3. Raise public awareness about mental health and reentry issues that veterans and their families face.

After technical peer review of the submitted proposals, WBV awarded seven academic medical centers with multiyear grants to begin activities in 2010 (Tanielian, Martin, & Epley, 2014). The seven grantees were:

- Duke University Veteran Culture and Clinical Competencies (V3C)
- Emory University—Emory's Veterans Program (EVP)
- Massachusetts General Hospital—Home Base Program
- Rush Medical Center—Road Home Program
- University of California, Los Angeles (UCLA)—Nathanson Family Resilience Center (NFRC)
- University of Michigan Depression Center—Military Support Programs and Networks (M-SPAN
- Weill Cornell Medical College Department of Psychiatry (Tanielian, Martin, & Epley, 2014).

With the award of the 2010 grants to university medical centers, WBV also engaged the RAND Corporation as WBV's performance monitoring center. In this capacity, RAND worked with the Robert R. McCormick Foundation, MLB, and the Steering Committee to facilitate engagement among grantees and sharing of best practices and lessons learned across the initiative. WBV held several all-grantee meetings throughout the course of the initiative (in New York City [NYC] in November 2011, which kicked off grantees' activities and RAND's performance-monitoring work, and in May 2013 and 2014 to discuss sustainability, fundraising, partnership-building, and strategy to take programs to the next level).

Throughout Phase I and Phase II, RAND collected data quarterly from grantees on their activities and progress, including information on the individuals receiving clinical services, partnership development, outreach and dissemination activities, education and training efforts, and challenges and goals. The RAND team also conducted quarterly calls with each grantee to discuss program activities and progress.

Beyond performance assessments for quarterly reports, the RAND team regularly engaged with grantees to keep abreast of program activities and enable coordination across the WBV initiative. For example, the RAND team conducted site visits to each grantee and convened all grantees on bimonthly phone calls to foster cross-grantee collaboration and discuss various topics related to program improvement and development (messaging, partnership development, training, engagement, and evaluation measures). Throughout Phase I and Phase II, RAND's role during the calls and meetings was primarily one of facilitation, analytic support, and administrative support. Working-group discussions concentrated on sharing common practices and themes across WBV and discussing emerging challenges and possible ways to resolve them. Groups also discussed the broader military and veterans' mental health systems and opportunities for advancement through partnership both within and outside WBV.

In 2014, RAND released a report on the initiative and its activities and impact (Tanielian, Martin, & Epley, 2014). The report covered the range of WBV activities raising awareness, conducting research, training providers and organizations, and delivering direct mental health services to service members, veterans, and their families. In summary, between 2010 and 2012, WBV partners provided clinical services (including screening, referral, and treatment) to more than 3,600 individuals, networked with 188 organizations, and conducted 228 training sessions or workshops to build new skills and capacities among veterans, organizations that serve them, and community-based providers. The report also offered insights on lessons learned from Phase I, including the need to develop public-private partnerships and enhance sustainability of the initiative. RAND also published a related report on public-private partnerships aimed at delivering mental health care to veterans and their families (Pedersen et al., 2015). The report integrated insights from RAND's review of WBV activities, identified key elements of successful public-private partnerships, and offered recommendations for improving the capacity and impact of public-private partnerships.

Phase II WBV Activities (2013–2016)

Building on the objectives and progress of the previous grant period, WBV issued another invitation-only request for proposals to six of the seven funded sites from the prior phase. One site was not asked to reapply based on concerns about progress and impact. The site had struggled with reaching veterans and attracting them into services and did not have strong partnership connections with organizations to facilitate recruitment or dissemination of training.

In releasing the Phase II funding opportunity, WBV asked its partner sites to focus their next wave of activities specifically on developing public-private partnerships and improving their programs' long-term sustainability and replicability. With a staggered start to funding grantees based on the timing of the previous grant cycle and review of proposals, Phase II of the initiative began on October 1, 2013. In Phase II, WBV provided funding to V3C, EVP, M-SPAN, the Home Base Program, the Road Home Program, and UCLA NFRC. In addition, a new site was added: the Steven A. Cohen Military Family Clinic (MFC) at New York University (NYU) Langone. We briefly describe these sites, highlighting how each used WBV funding to support its efforts.

Emory's Veterans Program

EVP is based in the Emory University Department of Psychiatry and offers free clinical treatment for post-9/11 veterans and their family members in Georgia and the southeastern United States. Through its own expansion efforts, EVP is now housed within a separate facility that colocates treatment services with neuroimaging capabilities and the sleep disorder clinic. This new space allowed EVP to create dedicated areas and hire additional staff to deliver treatment to veterans struggling with PTSD. EVP's clinical care services feature a range of treatment options for psychological disorders, including its state-of-the-art Virtual Reality Exposure therapy for PTSD.

With the support of WBV, EVP also developed a program to train community-based mental health providers to offer EBTs. EVP partnered with the Star Behavioral

Health Providers (SBHP) program to bring its training approach and registry management to the state of Georgia. Through SBHP, training is offered in three tiers: Tier One introduces military culture; Tier Two provides an overview of some behavioral health issues that service members and veterans may face; and Tier Three teaches clinical skills that focus on EBT. For Georgia, EVP selected PE therapy as the EBT for its Tier Three training.

The EVP-SBHP partnership is focused specifically on increasing its impact by training providers throughout Georgia in military cultural competency and evidence-based practices and by helping ensure that clinicians are locally available to serve veterans, service members, and their families. EVP also planned to use Phase II funding to expand the structure and format of the three-tier SBHP program to include something it refers to as Tier Four. This expansion incorporated structured, intensive workshop trainings on PE therapy coupled with follow-on regular clinical supervision to achieve certification. EVP further sought to expand the reach and impact of Tier Four by recruiting some providers to become additional trainers and supervisors for individuals within EVP's clinical settings and partnered with fellow WBV sites to offer these services to providers in those settings as well. The Tier Four program extended providers' prior training work in PE and prepared senior clinicians to supervise newer providers of PE—thereby extending capacity to train even more providers in the use of PE. To date, EVP staffers have trained providers and supervisors at Home Base and the Road Home Program and continue to work toward training a national network of PE consultants to improve access to EBT of PTSD across the United States. In 2015 and 2016 alone, EVP treated 344 veterans free of cost and trained 688 mental health providers. Of the mental health providers trained during this time frame, nine completed the Tier Four program designed by Emory by the end of 2016.

Duke University Veteran Culture and Clinical Competencies (Duke VC3) Program

Together, the Duke University Evidence-Based Practice Implementation Center and the Center for Child and Family Health founded the V3C program. Duke V3C does not provide direct clinical services to veterans and their families; instead, the program focuses solely on training and supplemental implementation activities for community-based providers (Tanielian, Martin, & Epley, 2014). During WBV Phase I, and based on its prior work in improving the delivery of mental health care in community settings, Duke VC3 developed intensive training models for organizations of providers. For example, Duke's VC3 Learning Series trains teams of four to eight staff members within community provider groups on military culture competency over the course of six monthly modules. Also, Duke V3C implemented the Breakthrough Series Collaborative through a yearlong pilot program that aimed to enhance community mental health care for veterans, service members, and families using a practice improvement model oriented to accomplishing the goals of participating provider groups (Murphy & Fairbank, 2013). In addition to these intensive models, Duke V3C also conducts various other training sessions, including webinars on various issues affecting veterans, service members, and their families.

Duke VC3 has used WBV support to focus on capacity-building efforts designed to improve competency among clinical and social-service providers throughout North Carolina and beyond. Duke VC3 continued to implement the Breakthrough Series Collaborative and the V3C Learning Series to train community teams across the United States using virtual and web-based techniques. In addition, Duke VC3 created the Learning Communities program to adapt the Resource Parenting Curriculum to incorporate educational materials for those delivering the curriculum to enhance their understanding of military families and caregivers on deployment-related issues. Duke VC3 also created the Learning Collaborative program on Cognitive Processing Therapy, designed to deliver intensive training and supervision to clinicians to deliver the evidence-based therapy in their own settings. VC3 also created a stronger partnership of veteran-serving organizations, helped empower peer navigators, and is now also serving as a partner in the NC Serves initiative, which links veteran-serving organizations across the state to work more effectively and collaboratively.

Red Sox Home Base Program

Based in Boston, Massachusetts, the Home Base program offers treatment for the mental health needs of post-9/11 service members, veterans, and families in New England. The Red Sox Foundation and Massachusetts General Hospital partnered to found Home Base, and both are key supporters of the grantee's outreach efforts, services, and research for veterans with PTSD and traumatic brain injuries. Home Base provides a range of clinical services to local service members, veterans, and families through face-to-face care at the hospital. Home Base also offers referral services to veterans at local universities and colleges throughout New England. In addition to in-person treatment, Home Base has increased the number of veterans and families served and extended its geographic reach through its telemedicine program and its training offerings. As the Home Base program has grown and evolved, it has also changed its physical footprint and locations. The ability to build new clinical space has enabled the program to create veteran- and family-friendly clinical spaces that can colocate and integrate multiple areas of clinical focus for veterans with PTSD and TBI.

With Phase II funding, Home Base increased the community capacity in New England by creating the Home Base Training Institute, which serves as a training hub for community providers serving the mental health needs of OIF/OEF veterans, service members, and families, and a Network Development Program, which developed partnerships and institutionalized clinical referral relationships with VA and community providers. These initiatives focus on extending access to evidence-based care and developing public-private partnerships.

The training institute was set up to include a four-level tiered curriculum focused on educating community providers, raising awareness, and enhancing support of post-9/11 service members, veterans, and military families. Each tier of the curriculum increases the level of intensity and engagement. The Tier One offerings include online training and resources; Tier Two includes in-person lectures, presentations, and outreach events conducted by faculty or veteran peer outreach coordinators; and Tier Three consists of two targeted online courses (four sessions each) with detailed curriculum materials and faculty interaction. The final level, Tier Four, includes a pilot project to offer a medium-intensity training and consultation model in PE for PTSD to community providers throughout New England.

The Home Base program continues to rely on the strong support of the Red Sox Foundation and has deepened its collaborative relationship with the VA, particularly the Boston VA Medical Center. Training sessions have also helped build capacity at other WBV sites and reached more than 20,000 learners (community-based providers of different types) throughout the nation. In addition to its work in expanding community-based capacity, Home Base provided outpatient services through its own direct clinical services to 459 veterans and 154 family members in 2014 and 2015 alone.

Military Support Programs and Networks

The University of Michigan Depression Center and Department of Psychiatry offer a range of mental health research and support programs for veterans, service members, and families. These programs make up M-SPAN, which operates six main programs, which are funded in whole or in part by WBV:

1. The Buddy-to-Buddy program is a peer partnership model that connects volunteer veteran mentors with service members to help them address various issues and link them to community resources. This program is a flagship effort for M-SPAN and the Michigan National Guard.
2. HomeFront Strong is an eight-week program for military and spouses on resiliency, relationship-building, self-care, and coping (M-SPAN, n.d.-b).
3. In partnership with the Student Veterans of America, Peer Advisors for Veteran Education (PAVE) matches veteran student mentors and mentees at Michigan colleges and universities. With additional funding from Bristol Myers Squibb Foundation, the PAVE program is now on more than 42 college campuses in the United States.
4. The Military Family Support Forum is a free program for OIF/OEF/OND veteran and military family members to participate in facilitated discussions on a range of relevant topics (University of Michigan, n.d.).
5. Strong Military Families is a ten-week program for military parents and children that teaches family resilience strategies, coping skills, and relationship-building and connects participants with other military families and programs (M-SPAN, n.d.-c).
6. In partnership with the Yellow Ribbon Program for the Michigan Army and Air National Guard, the Deployment Cycle Support offers workshops and training

for service members and their families on parenting, relationships, and communication (M-SPAN, n.d.-a).

In addition to these programs, M-SPAN convened the military family support community through three different summits, including the Michigan Summit on Military Families in 2011, National Research Summit on Reserve Component Military Families in 2013, and the National Summit on Military and Veteran Peer Programs. These summits aimed to extend the reach of research, treatment, and services for service members, veterans, and their families by facilitating the sharing of best practices, identifying knowledge gaps, and facilitating new relationships among partners.

With Phase II funding, M-SPAN created the Training Assistance Center to identify, train, and supervise community partners to deliver M-SPAN programs in their clinics and practices. Through the assistance center, M-SPAN aims to offer intensive training and create manuals and training videos for replication of all its programs. In Phase II of the initiative, M-SPAN also aims to expand the geographic reach of program offerings by collaborating with new partners throughout the State of Michigan. For example, MSPAN built a partnership with Easterseals Michigan to expand use of its military family support programs like Homefront Strong.

New York University Langone Cohen Military Family Clinic

In partnership with the VA New York Harbor Healthcare System, the Steven A. Cohen MFC at NYU Langone Medical Center offers free mental health care for service members, veterans, and families in the NYC area. The MFC is a suite of dedicated offices and treatment space within the NYU Langone Department of Psychiatry. MFC clinicians work directly with the Manhattan VA and other community partners to offer warm hand-offs, referrals, and clinical services in specialty areas, including alcohol and substance abuse, grief and loss, readjustment issues, parenting concerns, and children's behavioral or academic problems (NYU Langone Health, n.d.).

The MFC also offers tele–mental health for veterans and families throughout the state of New York. WBV funded the center's dual-diagnosis program for veterans, service members, and their family members with addiction and co-occurring mental health issues (NYU Langone Health, n.d.). The MFC also offers therapy for military families and children, couples therapy, and parenting support workshops (NYU Langone Health, n.d.).

With Phase II funding, the MFC sought to expand service offerings to treat more veterans, service members, and families by incorporating a dual-diagnosis treatment program for veterans struggling with substance use problems. The center employs a harm-reduction model to work with clients on reducing their substance use and to help integrate services to address both the substance use and mental health problems affecting the veteran and his or her family. To serve this community, the MFC expanded its relationships with the other service providers within NYC, including as part of the NYC Serves collaborator model. The MFC continues to operate in close coordination (and relies heavily on a bidirectional referral relationship) with the Manhattan VA medical center. To facilitate this relationship, the MFC has a part-time staff person from the Manhattan VA who coordinates referrals and care for MFC patients. The MFC continues to offer other direct clinical services to veterans and their family members using a short-term model of care, meaning most patients are seen at the clinic for less than a month before they are referred to other settings for follow-up care. Since being awarded the WBV grant, the MFC treated a total of 123 veterans and families in the dual-diagnosis program through 2016. Outside the WBV funding, the MFC is also engaged in several research trials related to veterans with PTSD and TBI and is part of the expanding network of clinics under the Cohen Veteran Network (CVN, described in Chapter Four).

Road Home Program at Rush University

Based in Chicago, Illinois, Rush University's Road Home Program provides clinical services for OIF/OEF veterans, service members, and their families. The grantee also offers a range of training offerings, including tiered training courses on MST and military culture competency for health care providers and family caregivers, which are offered in collaboration with Health & Disability Advocates. Road Home also partners with local colleges and universities to embed modules on PTSD, TBI, and MST into formal degree programs for health care providers and other professionals. Road Home aims to use the Families OverComing Under Stress (FOCUS) and TeleFOCUS (videoconferencing) models, developed at UCLA NFRC, to train community providers that serve military families.

Road Home sought Phase II funding to expand offerings in an array of areas, including MST, mental health treatment, TBI care coordination, specialized services for children, employer engagement, and wraparound services. In the second phase of the initiative, the grantee also sought to expand the geographic reach of its offerings; enhance partnerships with VA Medical Centers, Illinois Joining Forces, and other key veterans and military organizations; and expand capacity of partner providers to offer evidence-based services and treatment for service members, veterans, and families at their own sites. The Road Home Program continues to work closely within the Chicago area to train and educate community-based providers on the issues that face veterans and their families. As part of these efforts, the Road Home team partnered with the UCLA site to bring FOCUS to Chicago by getting their providers trained in the FOCUS model (described below) and equipped to then train other providers on how to use FOCUS and incorporate it into their own settings.

Original funding from WBV helped Rush University establish dedicated treatment space within its Department of Psychiatry. Because of increasing demand and additional support from the Wounded Warrior Project (WWP, as part of the Warrior Care Network [WCN], described in Chapter Four), Road Home was able to expand its treatment capacity and acquire a new physical location.

University of California, Los Angeles–Welcome Back Veterans Nathanson Family Resilience Center

UCLA NFRC's mission is to improve the psychological health and resilience of veterans, service members, and their families, and the program takes a family-centered approach to education and clinical services. UCLA NFRC has developed replicable models for treating military and veteran families. One such model is the FOCUS Prevention Program, which promotes resilience among military families. UCLA NFRC has leveraged technology to target military families and deliver training courses. For example, UCLA NFRC has used geographic information system technology to locate military families in California and offer care in their areas using mobile applications, telehealth, and social media. In addition, UCLA NFRC offers a video-telehealth home visiting intervention version of FOCUS–Early Childhood (through TeleFOCUS). UCLA NFRC has also collaborated with UCLA Health System to create Operation Mend-FOCUS, which provides surgical patients and families with web-based mental health care.

In Phase II, UCLA NFRC sought to increase the geographic reach of training offerings and position itself to collaborate with partners as a center for expertise on training and evaluation. UCLA NFRC has trained other providers across the United States to implement FOCUS training in their communities, including WBV grantee Rush University. The center's stated objective was to develop high-quality, accessible, family-centered behavioral health services within existing communities and systems of care for military-connected children and their families. A second objective of the center's Phase II efforts was to promote the integration of family-centered behavioral health into organizations that serve female veterans and recovering warriors with PTSD and TBI. Like the EVP, UCLA worked with SBHP to deliver three tiers of training for service professionals in California, and their unique contribution to Tier Three training was to train providers on FOCUS to enhance resilience and mitigate psychological distress among military and veteran families. During their work in Phase II, UCLA and SBHP reached more than 650 unique participants and trained 41 providers in the FOCUS model. They also expanded partnerships to reach a number of organizations within and outside California, including the Road Home Program at Rush and with the Canadian Armed Forces.

In addition to their focus on training more service providers in the FOCUS model, UCLA also used the WBV funding to further expand the availability of family resilience services via telehealth and mobile applications. These resources have also been integrated into UCLA's Operation Mend program for veterans with PTSD and TBI.

Performance Monitoring and Network Engagement

Throughout Phase II, RAND continued its performance-monitoring (regular reporting requirements, hosting conference calls, and conducting site visits). In addition,

WBV partner sites continued to gather in person and by phone to reflect on accomplishments; share lessons learned; and brainstorm on how to improve and expand WBV's public-private partnerships, sustainability, and replicability.

During in-person annual meetings in Washington, DC (in 2013, 2014, and 2015), WBV site representatives met with agency and policymaking officials, including those from DoD and VA, as well as those on Capitol Hill. A major theme during these discussions was WBV's relationship with VA. At the local level, there had been varying degrees of success across initiative partners with respect to formalizing relationships with the VA. Up through 2014, there was heavy emphasis on trying to establish formal public partnership agreements with the VA Central Office and with individual medical centers. Grantees devoted significant effort to informing their local VA Medical Center leadership about their work, noting that the initiative's clinical services for service members, veterans, and families are paid for through philanthropic funding. While the grantees will bill insurance if the individuals have it, WBV seeks to provide free services. The WBV partners also highlighted their efforts in expanding provider capacity and raising awareness. A summary of these activities is included later in this chapter.

WBV Areas of Emphasis

In Phase II of the WBV initiative, grantees focused their services on maximizing impact and aligning with the WBV aim of establishing sustainable programs that support the mental health needs of service members, veterans, and families through public-private partnerships. Main WBV areas of emphasis are expanding the provider base and competency, raising awareness, promoting help-seeking, delivering clinical services, and creating referral networks. These are described next.

Expanding Provider Base and Competency

Through a range of structured training and education offerings, WBV grantees sought to increase the pool of providers who are comfortable with and competent at providing mental health care for service members, veterans, and their families. WBV grantees' training efforts changed in focus and emphasis from the inception of the initiative. In Phase I, training became increasingly important over time. In Phase II, grantees continued to emphasize education and training as central components of their strategies for expanding local and regional capacity and promoting the replication of their approaches and activities. In total, since the inception of WBV, grantees have offered 564 training sessions that were taken by more than 29,000 learners.

WBV training courses ranged in intensity and focus over time. About one-half of these sessions train health care providers, some are offered in series, and most offer continuing education units for participation. Other training sessions aim to educate service members and veterans, students, community members, families, friends, and legal professionals serving military populations. More than one-half of the individual training sessions are low-intensity (90 minutes or less). Approximately one in four of the training sessions are medium-intensity (between 91 minutes and eight hours), and about one in five training sessions are high-intensity (more than eight hours). The vast majority of training sessions are offered in person (between 76 percent and 91 percent each reporting period). Telephone and online training sessions are the next–most-common training modes. Grantees also offer sessions via various combinations of in-person, online, telephone, and videoconference modes. Across the initiative, WBV grantees have leveraged their own expertise in EBT modalities (e.g., PE from EVP, Cognitive Processing Therapy from Duke, FOCUS from UCLA and Road Home) to increase the number of mental health providers who are also trained to deliver these treatments. A hallmark of these training efforts has been the use of supervision and supported implementation for their practice settings.

Raising Awareness and Promoting Help-Seeking

Throughout Phase II, WBV sites dedicated resources to outreach and dissemination efforts to increase awareness about mental health issues and program services and encourage help-seeking. To promote services, grantees have participated in community events; organized activities for veterans, service members, and their families; met with key stakeholders; and sent information about program offerings to various target audiences both online and in person. Over the course of implementing their programs, each grantee reported on the importance of a continued emphasis on spreading the word about not only the need among veterans and their families but also the availability of their programs. Some of the WBV sites reported that they partnered with other veteran supporting organizations (e.g., Student Veterans of America) to disseminate information and recruit individuals into trainings and clinical services. Sites varied in how much they invested in these activities; some were able to leverage media and local celebrities to help. Many of the programs also hired veterans as peer outreach specialists—helping engage other veterans but also offering peer-based support during service delivery. In the regular coordination calls, WBV sites reported that these peer specialists were critical members of their teams, helping build trust with the community and improve the cultural sensitivity within their sites.

Grantees regularly engaged in outreach activities to encourage target populations to seek WBV program services and take part in research studies. Since the inception of WBV, grantees reported conducting more than 1,170 outreach activities. Such activities include attending meetings with VA and DoD, local Reserve/Guard entities, and veteran service organizations. In addition, grantees have used social media, information booths, radio advertisements, and flyers to reach veterans, service members, and their families.

With the dual aims of raising public awareness about WBV programs and mental health and reducing stigma surrounding mental health treatment–seeking, grantees also reported that they had conducted nearly 2,000 distinct dissemination activities since the inception of WBV. Across the sites, the purposes of dissemination activities ranged from relationship-building to raising public awareness. The scale of events also varied, including meetings with small numbers of representatives from federal and local organizations and large community events intended for hundreds of individuals and many organizations.

During Phase II, most grantees' dissemination activities were designed to promote the training and services offered. Some examples of dissemination activities focused on training are calls and meetings with local university medical schools and health care providers. Grantees also interacted with other training organizations, such as SBHP, to collaborate on dissemination of training opportunities. Dissemination activities that sought to promote clinical services have included meeting with veteran service organizations and targeted discussions about offerings for female veterans, student veterans, and homeless veterans. Another aim of dissemination activities that was less frequently reported was sharing program models for replication. With this goal in mind, grantees met with universities and community colleges, Army National Guard and Reserve offices, and various veteran- and military-oriented organizations to discuss extending and replicating program models.

Dissemination activities have targeted specific populations with specified goals to share program information and promote engagement with organizations and individuals. Grantees' dissemination activities that focused on fundraising included benefit dinners to raise awareness and funding for programs that assist homeless veterans, meetings with various philanthropic organizations, and a 5K race. Dissemination activities that targeted the general public included participating in Veterans Day activities, giving keynote speeches at community college graduations, and offering radio interviews and public service announcements. To reach the research community, grantees have been very active in sharing studies and findings at conferences and summits across the United States and internationally. In pursuit of enhanced public-private partnerships, grantees have met with representatives from federal and local VA offices to share program offerings and effects and to discuss opportunities for collaboration.

Delivering Clinical Services

Four of the seven WBV sites deliver clinical care services directly to veterans and their families through individual or group therapy. These grantees reported using evidence-based or evidence-informed therapeutic interventions in clinical services for service members, veterans, and families. Two others offer nonmedical evidence-based or evidence-informed support services to families. Each of the four sites that delivered clinical services also prioritized gathering self-reported patient outcome data to track clinical progress and inform treatment decisionmaking. While the sites also reside within academic medical settings, they varied in their use of specific measures, but each maintained a focus on evaluating clinical progress as a key component of tracking its impact.

Although WBV highlights veterans in its title, the initiative serves high numbers of service members and families as well. Since the initiative's inception, WBV grantees provided clinical services to a total of 915 active component service members, 3,771 veterans, 901 Reserve/Guard members, and 5,146 family members in the form of screening, referrals, and treatment or care—for a total of 10,733 individuals. Of these, 4,131 received screening or precare services; 845 were referred for treatment or care at other clinics or organizations; and 5,757 have received treatment or care in one of the four WBV sites.

In addition to direct clinical services, grantees also provided nonclinical offerings, such as peer support services, parenting workshops, and facilitated discussions aimed at skill-building, resiliency, and wellness (Tanielian, Martin, & Epley, 2014).

Ripple Effect: Services Provided by Community-Based Providers Trained by WBV

At the end of Phase II, Duke VC3 began reporting the ripple effects of training providers who offer clinical services in the community. Duke VC3 reported services delivered to veterans and their family members by providers from the Center for Child and Family Health who completed their Cognitive Processing Therapy training course. In total, trained providers from the Center for Child and Family Health screened 15 veterans and one family member. In addition, at the time of reporting, four veterans and one family member were receiving services from trained providers from the Center for Child and Family Health. These numbers represent just one program that completed Duke VC3's course but offer a sense of the reach of the grantee's training efforts. Future tracking like this will be valuable in conveying the effects of Duke VC3 and other WBV grantees.

Addressing Unique Issues

In recognition of the myriad of issues that veterans and their families face and in addition to clinical services for PTSD, depression, and anxiety, many WBV sites developed other clinical services and training courses that focus on specific mental health issues and certain populations of service members, veterans, and families. Supplementing specialized options offered in DoD, VA, and community systems of care, WBV grantees have offered clinical services and training courses specifically oriented toward such issues as TBI, MST, and co-occurring substance use disorders and toward such groups as military families and female veterans. The remainder of this section highlights some efforts that grantees have undertaken in these areas.

Traumatic Brain Injury

Several WBV programs offer services specifically focused on veterans and service members with TBI. Throughout Phase I of the initiative, WBV grantees cited challenges with service eligibility for veterans with both PTSD and TBI. In an effort to overcome this challenge, improve service delivery, and ensure that patients are covered throughout the continuum of care, grantees strategically formed new partnerships with organizations that offer care for patients who need additional therapy for PTSD and TBI. Grantees' efforts to partner with organizations to improve mental health care for service members with TBI continued into Phase II. The Road Home Program offers TBI screening for psychological effects associated with the injury (Road Home Program, n.d.). If advanced care is needed, Road Home also refers service members, veterans, and families to Rush University Medical Center TBI specialists (Road Home Program, n.d.).

In Georgia, EVP works with TBI specialists, accessing neurologists and physiologists as needed for treating veterans and service members with TBI (Emory Healthcare, n.d.-a). EVP also offers treatment for TBI through a range of offerings, including psychotherapy, pharmacotherapy, and other treatment options that may be helpful, such as cognitive rehabilitation, stress management, and sleep training (Emory Healthcare, n.d.-a).

UCLA NFRC has also conducted research and developed mobile health options to enhance TBI treatment. Specifically, UCLA NFRC created a mobile health application that is designed to enhance caregiver and behavioral health provider communication about combat-related PTSD and TBI. UCLA NFRC is also working to generate a prototype for a second mobile application that offers services for veterans and service members with PTSD and TBI. UCLA NFRC also conducted research in the field on adapting a treatment protocol for resilience training for military families of veterans with severe PTSD and TBI. Like UCLA NFRC, NYU Langone is also offering services aimed at addressing PTSD and TBI. In July 2015, the Home Depot Foundation awarded NYU Langone Medical Center a $1.5 million grant to spearhead the NYC mental health consortium to enhance PTSD and TBI diagnosis and treatment (NYU Langone Health, 2015). Home Base also offers clinical services and referrals for service members and veterans with TBI.

Military Sexual Trauma

MST is another area in which grantees offer specialized services. For instance, Road Home offers clinical services and training for health care providers on MST treatment. The Road Home Program has also met with sexual assault response coordinators and held sexual assault awareness events and meetings with key community stakeholders working in the field. These efforts are aimed at increasing outreach and disseminating information about new psychological services offered to service members and veterans who have experienced MST. Similar to Road Home's efforts to treat service members and veterans who have experienced MST, EVP offers treatment for MST through its various clinical service offerings. It also offers focused treatment to help service members deal with haunting memories, anxiety, and depression that they may experience as a result of MST (Emory Healthcare, n.d.-b).

Co-Occurring Substance Abuse Problems

As described earlier, NYU Langone seeks to address the mental health and substance use issues of service members, veterans, and their families in the NYC metropolitan area through clinical care and research (NYU Langone Health, n.d.). NYU Langone's mental health and substance use program is confidential and free for service members, veterans, and families, which helps fill a gap in care for those who may not be eligible or are uncomfortable seeking care from VA, DoD, or other systems of care (NYU Langone Medical Center, 2014a). NYU Langone's Dual Diagnosis Program offers individual and group psychotherapy, medication management, and adjunctive therapies, such as mindfulness training and meditation (NYU Langone Medical Center, 2014b).

Military and Veteran Families

All grantees offer services that touch military and veterans' families. As discussed earlier, family members are the largest cohort receiving clinical services. A number of programs are aimed at serving military and veterans' families. UCLA NFRC's training for health care providers and other professionals on FOCUS aims to boost family resilience through strategies and skill-building (UCLA NFRC, n.d.-a). UCLA NFRC's focus program is offered in a specialized program for early childhood, offered to non–active duty OIF/OEF/OND veteran, Guard, or Reserve service members and their families with children ages 3 to 6. The program seeks to facilitate improved parent-child relationships and build effective parenting, problem-solving, and stress management skills (UCLA NFRC, n.d.-b).

Duke V3C's Breakthrough Series Collaborative was a two-year training program that sought to enhance North Carolina's mental health services for military families and children (Duke Evidence-Based Practice Implementation Center, 2015). The V3C Breakthrough Series Collaborative builds health care providers' knowledge, skills, and abilities to treat military families and informs them on methods for effective mental health treatment and models for engagement for ensuring military families' well-being and resilience through deployments and over time (Duke Evidence-Based Practice Implementation Center, 2015).

M-SPAN also has several services and activities aimed at mental health needs of military families. M-SPAN's HomeFront Strong offers group resilience therapy for post-9/11 service members and veterans and their spouses and partners in a free, eight-week course. With a focus on creating positive relationships, learning self-care, and coping skills, HomeFront Strong emphasizes resiliency among military and veteran couples (M-SPAN, n.d.-b). To facilitate participation in HomeFront Strong, M-SPAN offers free meals and child care, a children's program, and a teen program for participants (M-SPAN, n.d.-b). M-SPAN's Strong Military Families Program is a ten-week program for military parents and children that seeks to support family resiliency (M-SPAN, n.d.-c). To overcome barriers to care and facilitate access, the program is offered both as a multifamily group therapy and through mailed written materials (M-SPAN, n.d.-b).

Home Base offers a number of services for military families, including the 3-Generation Model of treatment, which seeks to ensure that service members and veterans and their entire families receive mental health screening and treatment if needed (Home Base Veteran and Family Care, n.d.). Home Base encourages family members to be part of service members' and veterans' treatment and care coordination (Home Base Veteran and Family Care, n.d.).

Female Veterans

Grantees have conducted outreach to specific subpopulations, including to female veterans. Grantees have reached out to female veterans through events offered by SheForce, coordinating with county jails and county family courts to help with counseling and mental health treatment for female veterans, and working with local organizations aimed at serving homeless female veterans.

Both grantees and community stakeholders are recognizing this group's unique challenges. UCLA NFRC has developed a new focus on female veterans in Los Angeles County and has developed a training curriculum for female veterans who are pregnant or mothers of infants. UCLA NFRC has aimed to disseminate this program online and use curriculum development to inform expanded programming for homeless and at-risk female veterans and their children.

Home Base has been working with VA to establish a model of care for female veterans and plans to focus on that area of care going forward. NYU Langone works with a large number of female veterans, has worked with the Manhattan VA's office for female veterans, and also works with Service Women's Action Network, a community group that advocates for female service members and veterans. NYU Langone emphasizes female veterans' services and options, including child care and women-only waiting rooms. In addition, M-SPAN has conducted a needs assessment to inform the design and development of programs for female veterans. Last, Rush worked to increase offerings oriented toward female veterans.

These examples of specified program services are just a sampling of WBV grantee efforts to meet the unique needs of service members, veterans, and their families. When specified services are not offered, grantees work to ensure that individuals get the care they need through care coordination and referrals. Beyond the populations specified, WBV grantees also have made efforts to reach out to student veterans (particularly M-SPAN), military caregivers (UCLA NCRF, M-SPAN, and Home Base), and homeless veterans (UCLA NCRF).

Creating Safety Nets: Referral Networks

In some respects, the WBV sites have served as safety nets, helping ensure that service members, veterans, and families receive appropriate mental health care. First, WBV filled gaps in coverage by serving veterans, service members, and family members who may be ineligible or unwilling to seek care at VHA, MHS, or other private/community health care systems. Offering low-cost and free care helps reach service members, veterans, and families who may have fallen through the cracks because of financial constraints. Grantees engaged such veterans, service members, and families through outreach and dissemination efforts, as well as clinical referrals from VHA, MHS, or private/community health care systems.

Second, WBV grantees also referred eligible patients to VHA, MHS, and private/community health care programs for long-term or more-intensive care, as needed. In this way, WBV's partnerships and the bidirectional referrals they offer help ensure that individuals have access to adequate mental health care from whatever system seems most appropriate.

Third, WBV's individual and collaborative efforts to raise awareness about mental health and reduce stigma associated with treatment-seeking aim to encourage service members, veterans, and families to understand their mental health options and pursue treatment as needed. Through these three main approaches, WBV services complement those offered through other systems of care. In addition, WBV services help ensure that veterans, service members, and families are informed about and comfortable within the network of care options available to them.

Summary

The WBV initiative offers a number of important insights for improving public-private partnerships and mental health care services for service members, veterans, and their families. Through training activities, delivery of direct mental health services, and efforts to improve outreach and dissemination, WBV grantees have enhanced MHS, VHA, and private systems of care. Since the initiative began in 2010 (and through 2016), WBV grantees have provided clinical services to a total of 915 active component service members, 3,771 veterans, 901 Reserve/Guard members, and 5,146 family members in the form of screening, referrals, and treatment or care—for a total of 10,733 individuals. In addition, grantees have provided training to 28,736 individuals. Attendees at the June 2014 all-grantee meeting reported that WBV rivaled VA training offerings in terms of number of sessions offered and number of individuals trained. Moreover, WBV outreach and dissemination activities have informed large numbers of individuals about mental health and encouraged them to seek mental health care if they need it.

In addition to these efforts, WBV has enhanced system capacity by providing specialized services for female veterans, service members and veterans with TBI, military and veteran families, service members and veterans with substance abuse and co-occurring issues, and service members and veterans who have experienced MST and by creating referral networks and local communities for collaboration. The WBV services focus on unique military and veteran populations help fill a gap in care for those who may not be eligible for or who are uncomfortable seeking care from MHS, VHA, or other systems of care.

The WBV initiative has made strides in serving service members, veterans, and families and in facilitating collaboration among systems of care in local communities. However, strategic efforts are needed to address challenges that MHS, VHA, and private systems of care face and to take advantage of opportunities that arise. Chapter Four describes the challenges and opportunities that exist in the military and veterans' health care landscape.

Understanding a Rapidly Emerging and Evolving Landscape

There are a number of emerging efforts that are likely to continue to change the mental health care service landscape for service members, veterans, and families. The increasing privatization of VA health care and the emergence of new collectives, such as the WCN and the CVN, may spur additional shifts in programs and policy and influence how the systems of care are able to absorb and address the demand for behavioral health care among veterans and their family members. Some of these issues are discussed here.

Increasing Use of Community Care for Veterans

Through the Veterans Choice Act and the emergence of such programs as Patient-Centered Community Care (PC3), VHA is becoming increasingly reliant on community-based sources of care. While the future of these programs is uncertain, key stakeholders and data indicate that VHA's reliance on private organizations to provide care for veterans will continue to increase (Greenberg et al., 2015). Through partnering with VHA as community care providers, private mental health programs may be eligible to become authorized providers under VA community care programs (through VA's purchased care contract provider networks), thereby enhancing their sustainability while helping improve access to high-quality care for veterans across the United States.

Warrior Care Network

Launched in January 2016, the WCN is a partnership between WWP and academic medical centers to form a national collective that will improve access to clinical care for service members and veterans with PTSD, TBI, and related conditions (Albin, 2016). The WCN grew out of ongoing discussions and relationships among four of the WBV sites: Emory Healthcare, Massachusetts General Hospital, Rush University Medical Center, and UCLA Health. Working collaboratively and in consultation with WWP, these clinical teams identified the need for a more intensive program to serve veterans with difficult-to-treat PTSD. The development of this effort was greatly accelerated not only by the personal connections among the project leaders at these sites but also through the ongoing interactions they maintained and nurtured through their WBV participation. The result is a nationally dispersed program that offers specialized, intensive, family-centered clinical services for veterans with mental health problems.

In total, WWP and its partners have invested $100 million in the initial three-year establishment of the WCN (WWP, n.d.). Service members and veterans are able to receive care from the WCN at no direct personal cost. However, for patients with insurance, WCN may bill their health plans so that the network funding can maximize the number of veterans treated (WWP, n.d.). Costs that are not covered by insurance are covered by WCN funds, so patients are not responsible for copays or other fees (WWP, n.d.).

WCN encourages cross-site collaboration and the sharing of lessons learned to improve processes and quality of care at each site (WWP, n.d.). In fact, these four academic medical centers worked to create a state-of-the-art medical record system and to incorporate patient-reported outcomes as a means of furthering measurement-based care practices. They also work collaboratively on training and supervising their providers, thus ensuring appropriate competencies in military and veteran culture and evidence-based practices. While the intake and referral process is centralized and coordinated, each site specializes in something slightly different. For example, the Road Home Program specializes in the treatment of MST; UCLA specializes in reconstructive surgical services in addition to mental health care, allowing referrals to individual sites to be tailored to the veteran's needs and geography. WCN works with VHA case management and care coordination staff members to recruit veterans and ensure their needs are met across the continuum of care, which may mean that a veteran is referred back to a VA provider for follow-up maintenance care after completion of the intensive program (WWP, n.d.). WCN aims to provide care for thousands of veterans (WWP, n.d.).

The Cohen Veteran's Network

With a donation of nearly $300 million, Steven A. Cohen founded CVN, which seeks to develop a national network of 25 clinics offering free mental health care for veterans and their families (Gordon, A. L., 2016). The program emphasizes services for post-9/11 veterans. Providing outpatient mental health care support in the short and medium terms, CVN's objective is to provide mental health services to 50,000 veterans by 2021 (Soule, 2016). As of mid-2017, CVN had opened in partnership with several clinics: Family Endeavors, Inc., in San Antonio and El Paso, Texas; Metrocare in Addison, Texas; NYU Langone Medical Center (a WBV funded site and original Cohen center); the University of Pennsylvania in Philadelphia, Pennsylvania;

Easterseals in Silver Spring, Maryland; and Cape Fear Valley in Fayetteville, North Carolina. In early 2017, CVN announced plans to expand further by selecting three new cities: Denver, Colorado; Los Angeles, California; and Killeen, Texas.

CVN clinics offer treatment to adults (veterans or other loved ones) and children. Each site has a dedicated team that includes not only clinicians but also outreach staff and case managers. Clinics may vary in terms of whether they have free-standing facilities or specialty clinics within larger settings, but each is expected to design a welcoming, family-friendly environment. As they join the network, CVN clinics will adopt standardized procedures and systems for tracking performance, which includes adoption of a common electronic health record (EHR) and cloud-based data warehouse. CVN operates on a franchisor-franchisee model, complemented by centralized leadership and infrastructure support across several domains, including training of providers and raising public awareness.

In addition to the outpatient mental health care services offered through CVN, $30 million will be used for the Cohen Veterans Bioscience cooperative's research on biomarkers and drug-based therapy for PTSD and TBI (Gordon, 2016).

Headstrong Project

Based at the Weill Cornell Medical College, the Headstrong Project is a relatively new program to offer confidential, pro bono EBT to post-9/11 combat veterans. Developed and implemented in NYC, the program has now expanded to other areas, including San Diego, California; Houston, Texas; Chicago, Illinois; Washington, DC; and Seattle, Washington. A veteran interested in services completes a centralized intake process and then an individual evaluation before being referred to one of the Headstrong providers in his or her area. While treatment plans are individually designed, Headstrong uses eye movement desensitization and reprocessing therapy, neurofeedback, and physical and social activities for patients. Headstrong depends on philanthropic support from individuals and foundations to make the care available to veterans. Weill Cornell and Headstrong envision expanding to 20 sites over the next several years.

Specialized Provider Registries

In addition to initiatives that provide direct clinical services, such as CVN and WCN, provider registries also seek to increase community care for veterans. Provider registries furnish service members, veterans, and their families with lists of health care providers who have participated in training on veteran and military culture or who wish to serve the population. While each registry is focused on meeting specific aims and serves a different geographic area, the registries have common objectives of enhancing the military and veteran sensitivity and skill sets of community providers and connecting these providers with service members, veterans, and families. The various offerings and activities are exemplified by a few programs with provider registries: AmericaServes, Give an Hour, and SBHP.

AmericaServes

AmericaServes offers an online platform for veterans, service members, and families to access services from health care providers. The initiative seeks to link service members and veterans with local programs and resources. Such programs and resources cover services in a wide spectrum of areas, including finances, fitness, employment, health care, housing, legal, and recreation. Within each service area, a range of services is provided. For example, the health care connections include links to community provider networks, equine therapy services, and military and veteran organizations providing various services, including clinical support services, peer engagement, and other offerings designed to improve health and wellness. AmericaServes has networks in the following states: New York, North Carolina, Pennsylvania, South Carolina, and Washington (AmericaServes, n.d.-b).

Give an Hour

Give an Hour offers a registry of behavioral health providers and alternative providers (offering such services as yoga and meditation) who have agreed to dedicate at least one hour a week of free behavioral health services to service members, veterans, and their families. The Give an Hour registry includes providers in all 50 states. As of August 2017, the Give an Hour registry included nearly 5,500 behavioral health providers covering a range of specialties (Give an Hour, n.d.-a). Service members, veterans, and families can search for providers using Give an Hour's online search tool. Those searching for services through the registry may also be guided by site administrators. Service members, veterans, and families needing additional services, including medication, may be referred to appropriate providers (Give an Hour, n.d.-b).

Star Behavioral Health Providers

SBHP offers a tiered training program for behavioral health providers offering instruction on military and veteran culture and evidence-based practices. The tiered training system is structured to increase providers' knowledge and skills as they progress through Tiers One, Two, and Three. Tier One introduces military culture (SBHP, n.d.-b); Tier Two provides an overview of some behavioral health issues that service members and veterans may face (SBHP, n.d.-c); and Tier Three teaches clinical skills that focus on EBT, including PE therapy for PTSD and Cognitive Processing Therapy (SBHP, n.d.-d).

In addition to its training offerings, SBHP manages online registries of nearly 900 providers who have participated in at least seven hours of training. Veterans, service members, and families can access the registries to find trained behavioral health providers in their communities. SBHP registries are offered in the following states: California, Georgia, Indiana, Michigan, New York, Ohio, Oregon, South Carolina, and Utah (SBHP, n.d.-a). SBHP is planning to add more states to its network (SBHP, n.d.-a).

Other Platforms and Provider Lists

In addition to AmericaServes, Give an Hour, and SBHP, there are a number of other provider registries or online platforms advertising access to mental health counseling for veterans. This includes such resources as Talk Space, Centerstone Military Services, The Soldier's Project, and Sound Off. One issue with these registries and platforms is the range of competencies and capacities of registered providers. Furthermore, most of these registries do not cover the expanse of the United States, including areas where provider shortages are acute. Even if they did, they would not solve the provider shortage issue. Such issues contribute to the complexity of the enduring challenges that the systems of care face, as described in the following section. We also know very little about the specific capabilities and quality of providers at the sites, which vary in terms of their description in publicly available materials.

Enduring Challenges

Each of the emerging initiatives designed to increase capacity of care for service members, veterans, and families faces a number of challenges. These include sustainability and dependence on philanthropy, negotiating third-party payments, and coordination and integration.

Sustainability Concerns with Respect to Reliance on Philanthropic Support

Public and philanthropic support for service members and veterans increased when the United States entered conflicts in Iraq and Afghanistan (Carter & Kidder, 2015). As a result of this swell of support, today there are more than 40,000 philanthropic organizations specifically focused on the veteran and military communities (Carter & Kidder, 2015). In the past, efforts have focused on improving coordination and communication to help service members, veterans, and their families access the services they need within the large set of public and philanthropic organizations. However, the overwhelming size of the service network is no longer the primary policy concern. Because of drawdowns in Iraq and Afghanistan, philanthropic support and government funding for service members, veterans, and military families' programs has already begun to decline (Chairman's Office of Reintegration: Veterans/Families/Communities, 2014). In 2011, the number of nonprofits specifically aimed at serving military and veteran community rose to its highest level, but this number has gradually decreased in recent years (Carter, 2012). Although support has begun to diminish, the need continues for programs to support the reintegration and mental health needs of service members, veterans, and their families (Chairman's Office of Reintegration: Veterans/Families/Communities, 2014). Consequently, a gap is emerging between supply of services and demand for support (Carter, 2012).

Private military and veterans' mental health programs have taken steps to improve their sustainability. One measure that some programs have used is changing their service models to continue to gain philanthropic support. Within the philanthropic realm, there is competition to gain recognition and a reputation for funding new ideas and occupying distinct niches in a given funding space (Fulton, Kasper, & Kibbe, 2010). Programs have responded to this need to establish unique services by changing their offerings to win grants. While this specialization may be helpful to certain groups of service members, veterans, and families who need these services, changing the program model may also negatively affect such groups as they seek to navigate the dynamic assortment of programs that are rebranding and shifting in their services and focus. On the program side, constant change to capture philanthropic support may result in a state of constant flux where programs are continually seeking to build and adjust capacity rather than bolster core competencies and develop partnerships. This model of constant change stresses both the people and the functioning of these organizations and fails to capitalize on quality and efficiency gains from establishing and adhering to a long-term vision and strategy.

In developing a shared vision and mission for providing military and veteran mental health care in a resource-constrained future, programs, including WBV grantees, must grow public-private partnerships as integral components of their operation in a system of systems. Such programs as WBV should also pursue sustainable revenue streams—e.g., third-party payments—that will enable them to build capacity and institutionalize their roles in the broader mental health system. In addition, expanding and fortifying the existing networks of partners will help the mental health field accomplish its shared goals.

Negotiating Third-Party Payments

Negotiating third-party payments may be one way in which private mental health programs, including WBV grantees, can improve their sustainability. While one of the attractions of private mental health care programs, such as WBV grantees, is the free care they offer, negotiating third-party payments for service members, veterans, and family members with insurance would allow private programs to stretch their funding further without hindering access to care.

Some grantees in the WBV initiative have found it challenging to complete the paperwork and processes required to become network providers in TRICARE, PC3, and VA Choice. Indeed, these networks have administrative requirements to ensure the quality of providers and care in their network. To enter the TRICARE, PC3, and VA Choice provider networks, health care programs and providers must work with the managed care support contractors that are assigned to various regions of the United States and abroad (TRICARE, 2016a). The managed care support contractors create provider networks, certify that programs and providers meet certain standards, and educate providers to ensure they provide quality care.

While the logistical and administrative requirements for establishing status as TRICARE, PC3, and Choice providers necessitates some effort from programs and providers, the investment in establishing the arrangement will offer dual benefits in program sustainability and access to high-quality mental health care for service members, veterans, and families.

Barriers to Coordination and Integration

MHS, VHA, and community/private systems of care operate mostly as independent structures. There are touch points for coordination, but these systems are far from integrated, resulting in isolated structures of care that can be difficult for patients to navigate. Reinforced by separate funding sources and established mechanisms, this "silo" structure fails to leverage partnerships to make gains in quality, effectiveness, or efficiency of mental health care provision. Instead, programs separately hone best practices in such areas as tele–mental health care, rural health care, and collaborative care, missing opportunities for shared learning. Systemic information-sharing is needed to facilitate coordinated, sustainable improvements to mental health care practices. Overcoming barriers to coordination and integration will require shared planning and development efforts and better coordination across systems of care and private initiatives, such as WBV.

Information-Sharing

Improving information-sharing can help foster partnerships and collaboration. However, the processes for it are constrained by various measures to keep personal information safe (Richardson & Asthana, 2006). Balancing the protection of patient confidentiality with the sharing of information is a major challenge in health care provision (Jenkins, 2014).

The technical aspects of information-sharing are important. IT systems can be useful facilitators for sharing information, but their use is also associated with concerns regarding the security of systems, data management and updating, and data storage processes (Jenkins, 2014). The compatibility of computer systems for accessing personal records will affect information-sharing capabilities (Richardson & Asthana, 2006). The successful use of electronic medical records for sharing information across organizations is also contingent on the accessibility of high-quality, standardized data (Gray et al., 2009). For effective information-sharing, such data must use a common system of clinical descriptors and be based on the same instrument tools for assessment (Gray et al., 2009). At present, DoD, the VA, WCN (which includes four of the seven WBV sites) and CVN (which includes one WBV site) all use separate, independent record-keeping systems. While there may be some overlap in the types of information and data they collect, the compatibility of their systems is unknown.

In addition to issues with technical systems, there are several other aspects of information-sharing that may hinder or facilitate coordination across systems of care. For example, there are a number of statutes and regulations that govern information-sharing processes (Richardson & Asthana, 2006). Mental health care programs must ensure that their processes and IT systems abide by this governance. In addition, the sufficiency of training and support for personnel to use information-sharing systems also has a bearing on the effectiveness of implementation (Richardson & Asthana, 2006). Personnel should also be well trained in assessment and data-sharing processes (Gray et al., 2009). Moreover, the timing and the appropriateness of shared information commonly affects the provision of person-centered care (Gondek et al., 2017). In summary, programs must ensure that information-sharing follows a number of guidelines for appropriateness and security that depend on both technical systems and personnel.

Response to the growing demand for multisector care coordination in the U.S. health care system provides a relevant example of how information can be shared across silos to improve the lives of vulnerable populations. There is evidence that behavioral and social factors have both short-term and long-term effects on health (Adler, Glymour, & Fielding, 2016), and a number of initiatives are under way to address those factors. The IOM has recommended a measure set on social determinants of health (SDoH) for health care organizations to include in their EHRs (IOM, 2014) and many are beginning to capture such data in EHRs. As a way to maximize patient-centered care as this movement continues, more and more organizations will be tracking and monitoring the various social and community services that patients use in addition to traditional medical services. Adoption of and tailoring of the IOM recommendations regarding which SDoH domains to include in shared databases is likely to create opportunities to integrate services across silos and systems and to improve care for veterans, service members, and their families.

A final point to note about information-sharing is the potential benefits of integration. As one of the most collaborative organizational relationships, integration is at the far end of the partnership spectrum for information-sharing (Richardson & Asthana, 2006). In integrated systems of care, the objective is to establish seamless, collaborative service provision, where colocated staff from different organizations work in teams on the same IT systems (Richardson & Asthana, 2006). Integration offers benefits for information-sharing and collaboration because so many aspects of workflow are communal, diminishing issues with technical and organizational compatibility. However, the integration model may not be feasible for all organizations. Therefore, organizations therefore seek to maximize information-sharing capabilities based on their objectives for collaboration and a range of factors that promote and constrain implementation.

Potential Opportunities

Despite enduring challenges, there are a number of ways in which systems of care and private programs can better coordinate. Although such programs often seek to distinguish themselves in the mental health field, they have many common objectives, processes, and challenges. Collaboration and sharing successful models for service delivery can help address shared challenges and improve sustainability of all organizations involved. There is also potential for major gains in efficiency and effectiveness by leveraging technology and implementing best practices.

Recognizing the mutual benefits of collaboration is the first step. The next crucial step is developing partnerships to cultivate and institutionalize collaboration. As this section explores, creating larger collaborative networks and maximizing the benefits of the environment of support for service members, veterans, and families may spur improvements in the organizational processes and outcomes of private programs, such as WBV.

Creating Larger Collaborative Networks

To improve impact and sustainability, collaborative networks, such as WBV, could continue to strengthen both their national and local partnerships. WBV grantees have seen the benefits of such network-building. On a local level, grantees have developed creative solutions to overcome barriers to care by working with partner organizations. For example, Home Base has partnered with Massachusetts State Troopers, who volunteer to drive veterans, service members, and families to their appointments so that transportation does not hinder access to care. On a national level, grantees have shared ideas, training models, and contacts and have advocated the value of these programs as initiatives. On both local and national levels, the WBV grantees' efforts to cultivate and grow partnerships have resulted in improved utilization and quality of services.

WBV grantees have also used their relationship with each other to expand their own capacities and collaboratively launch other efforts aimed at filling gaps. One example of this was the establishment of the WCN's Intensive Outpatient Program. In addition, WBV sites have worked to share expertise and capacity-building efforts, particularly around the use of peers and the adoption of a family systems–based approach. For example, the Duke V3C program worked with M-SPAN when it considered building a peer-based model for North Carolina; more recently, the Road Home Program and UCLA worked to bring FOCUS to providers in Illinois, first training Road Home providers and then opening up training to other community-based providers in the region. In addition to these collaborations within WBV, each site has worked to establish relationships and connections with other local or regional collaborative efforts designed to serve veterans and their families.

AmericaServes and America's Warrior Partnership are two examples of collaborative networks that have expanded and improved partnerships to better serve the military and veteran community. Both of these networks work at a regional or state level to connect community service providers with each other and with veterans to serve the holistic needs of the veteran community (AmericaServes, n.d.-a; America's Warrior Partnership, n.d.). Each uses a technology infrastructure and works with public and private organizations.

Along with WBV, AmericaServes, and America's Warrior Partnership, there is a vast range of national and local collaborative networks working to provide mental health care for service members, veterans, and military families. This includes the networks described earlier, as well as newer initiatives, such as the Warrior Wellness Alliance recently initiated by the George W. Bush Institute (George W. Bush Institute, 2017). These networks overlap and connect in various ways, with many organizations working with VHA, MHS, and common national and local partners. Collaborative networks can offer value to the greater mental health field through sharing lessons learned, best practices, and service models for replication.

Expanding and institutionalizing the connections within and across collaborative networks may improve sustainability of programs and create unique capabilities through the strategic combination of their core competencies (Bititci, Martinez, Albores, & Parung, 2004). To expand the existing networks, programs must reach out to form new connections with other networks and programs while developing relationships with existing partners. In addition, programs must invest in the mutual benefits of communication and synchronization to foster connectivity within growing collaborative networks. Once trust, commitment, and equity are established, these networks may realize the benefits of sharing risks and responsibilities and coordinated strategic planning for providing care to service members, veterans, and their families. Building better connectivity across networks will also help raise awareness of the offerings within. Through advocacy, outreach, and dissemination, extended collaborative networks can activate the public and gain stakeholder support and funding to sustain programs. Multisector networks will also benefit veterans by helping address multiple types of needs through complementary services, ultimately by creating efficiencies through a shared database to track needs and services used across programs and services. An electronic service record would potentially strengthen referrals and facilitate data-sharing as another means for advocacy and support.

Continuing Emphasis and Priority for the United States

Caring for service members, veterans, and their families should be a continuing priority for the United States. President Obama's steadfast support for veterans was clear through the growth of VA's budget, which expanded from $100 billion in FY 2009 (VA, 2015) to $170 billion in FY 2017 (VA, 2017). Presidential leadership, public support, and congressional oversight have pushed policymakers to improve mental health care for service members, veterans, and their families. Major policy initiatives, such as Obama's 2012 Executive Order, *Improving Access to Mental Health Services for Veterans, Service Members, and Military Families* (Obama, 2012), an additional 19 executive actions in 2014 to improve on the progress made in mental health care services since that 2012 Executive Order, and the development of Joining Forces and numerous other public and private programs have sought to transform systems of care to be better integrated, more collaborative, and standardized based on evidence-based practices. In addition, Congress has passed several key pieces of legislation in the past decade to improve a range of health care services for military- and veteran-affiliated populations.

The large number of sustained and developing initiatives that support and supplement these executive actions and legislation convey both the public and private dedication to improving services for service members, veterans, and their families. The financial and policy factors have created an environment of support for military and veterans' programs. Such an environment offers the critical resources and political backing to enact the types of policy and program improvements that are needed to overcome enduring challenges in the field. Military and veterans' mental health programs, including WBV, should seek to capitalize on such opportunities offered through legislation, funding, and community care programs. At the same time, however, it is worth noting that greater attention to the opportunity to use the continued interest in addressing veteran mental health needs as a mechanism to build and grow community-based support for all those living with mental health problems may provide a more sustainable approach over the long term as the nation works to bolster its ability to serve all of those with mental health problems.

Summary

Military and veterans' mental health systems face a number of challenges yet have a number of opportunities. These systems have developed many innovative solutions and collaborative networks that have helped meet the mental health needs of service members, veterans, and families. However, as public and philanthropic support shifts and resources become more constrained, programs, including WBV grantees, must continue learning and adapting to sustain their mental health service offerings and meet the demand for care. Negotiating third-party payment and expanding collaborative networks may help private mental health care programs, such as WBV, build capacity and impact going forward.

Current shifts in MHS, VHA, and community care systems have spurred positive changes, but more must be done to enhance mental health services. Improved use of telemedicine, IT, and public-private partnerships are auspicious approaches for bolstering mental health access and quality (Russell, 2010). Likewise, a number of new initiatives on the horizon hold promise for enhanced mental health care provision. Although there is no panacea for improving the mental health systems for care for service members, veterans, and their families, together, these policies and programs seeking to improve quality of and access to care may help overcome challenges within and across systems of care.

CHAPTER FIVE

Looking to the Future: Facilitating a System-of-Systems Approach

As discussed in the previous chapter, WBV is situated within a larger, more complicated set of systems of care that includes the federal systems of care we described in Chapter Two and the newer initiatives and clinical networks discussed in Chapter Four. Like these other entities, grantees in the WBV initiative share the goal of providing high-quality mental health care to service members, veterans, and their families. While WBV grantees have made significant efforts to build partnerships with national and local programs, they have operated independently from each other and independent of these other networks for the most part. There are several ways in which the grantees can work together more effectively and link to these other networks to meet their common objectives (such as how four of them formed the WCN), bolster relations with their network of partners, and increase their impact on service members, veterans, and families. This chapter examines the potential benefits of adopting a system-of-systems approach for those working in the nongovernmental sector to provide mental health services for service members, veterans, and their families. We provide a basic description of the system-of-systems approach and highlight how it might provide a useful framework for creating greater synergy within and among the various veteran mental health systems currently operating across the public and private sectors. In this section, we use the term *veteran mental health systems* to include specialized efforts led within the nongovernmental sector to expand capacity (WBV, WCN, CVN, SBHP, Give an Hour).

To outline how the current landscape of providers of mental health services for veterans and their families could enhance efficiency and quality, we first define the concept of a system-of-systems approach and then outline key attributes of how such a system can help the entities within the system learn, adapt, and improve their own services and sustainability. For each of these key attributes, we first describe the relevant characteristics and dimensions and then discuss how they might be applied by the WBV grantees and other entities within a system-of-systems approach for addressing the mental health needs of veterans and their families.

What Is a System-of-Systems Approach?

The system-of-systems approach conceptualizes the range of autonomous but inter-related organizations as components of a greater, multifaceted system (Rouse, 2012). There are four elements of a system-of-systems approach that are commonly associated with the concept: operational and managerial independence, geographic distribution, evolutionary development, and emergent behavior (when a number of individual entities collectively behave similarly as a result of environmental factors within their larger system) (Wickramasinghe, Chalasani, Boppana, & Madni, 2007). These elements align with WBV's structure and developments, making the system-of-systems approach a natural model for WBV and perhaps the other organizations within the nongovernmental sector as well.

A major advantage of the system-of-systems approach is that it conveys a sense of perspective on how programs work together to address cross-cutting policy problems and meet their shared missions (DeLaurentis & Callaway, 2004). There is no single director within a system of systems, and each involved entity participates in directing work-flows and influencing decisions (DeLaurentis & Callaway, 2004). Within the system-of-systems paradigm, each program must consider the broad spectrum of factors affecting other programs and clients in its network in order to maximize effectiveness of the model. This means that programs must coordinate with entities that may function outside their direct area of work (DeLaurentis & Callaway, 2004). Thus, within an effective system of systems, programs have to recognize that individual entities are less important than how they contribute to the higher-level network within which they operate (DeLaurentis & Callaway, 2004).

Key Elements of This Approach for Improving Quality and Sustainability

Emphasis on Learning Lessons, Continuous Performance Improvement, and Continuous Quality Improvement

The system-of-systems approach connects dispersed programs through communication, coordination, and infrastructure that support collaboration and a culture that is oriented toward holistic performance (DeLaurentis & Callaway, 2004). To facilitate such partnership, programs must emphasize continuous performance and quality improvement and establish a learning environment where individuals are empowered to solve problems and improve processes.

Robust data collection and sharing efforts are needed to inform process adaptation, quantify progress and success, and convey impact across systems of care. Developing and implementing common measures will assist in continuous performance and quality improvement for individual programs and the greater system of systems.

Development and Use of Common Measures

While services vary across the various nongovernmental efforts designed to serve veterans and their families, there are also many similarities. For example, most WBV grantees offer a range of training courses for different stakeholders on military and veteran topics. Furthermore, all grantees offer training courses for mental health providers on various related subjects, including psychotherapy approaches, military cultural competency, MST, and treatment for specific cohorts of service members, veterans, and families. WBV grantees have begun to develop a number of new training models and are working toward gathering evidence of their effects on participants' behavior. However, newer organizations and other entities offer similar trainings and activities. Thus, training efforts across all these various organizations are fragmented. While this has likely allowed innovation among independent organizations using different training approaches, it has likely also created some waste and inefficiency in the use of precious nonprofit funding. In fact, training development efforts across these various entities have functioned much like a natural experiment; organizations' efforts to train providers and other groups developed around the same time in different settings, and organizations have used distinct but comparable methods for training mental health care providers. However, unlike an experiment, common measures have not been used across the various efforts to capture the impact of individual and collective efforts on those who have participated in training. To adapt these efforts and methodically move the system of systems toward better practices, common measures are needed to evaluate inputs, outputs, outcomes, and impact. Furthermore, better-coordinated performance measurement and communication across the WBV initiative and across the nongovernmental systems may help each organization learn from others' experiences and adopt best practices. Beyond the WBV sites, this challenge extends to other clinical and training sites, where each likely has its own approach to whether and how to measure outcomes.

Adoption of Formal Continuous Performance Improvement and Continuous Quality Improvement Strategies

To facilitate a system-of-systems approach, two methods of performance management may be used to regularly monitor and adapt processes across disparate entities: continuous performance improvement (CPI) and continuous quality improvement (CQI). CPI is more focused on processes and service, while CQI emphasizes quality. Both approaches may assist the various veteran mental health systems of care in orienting personnel and processes toward being more adaptive.

CPI is the continuous evaluation and enhancement of health care processes and services to better meet patients' needs (Chestatee Regional Hospital, 2017). In regularly assessing workflows and health care personnel and patients' perceptions about their practices, programs gather data that can inform process changes and improve patient health outcomes (Chestatee Regional Hospital, 2017). CPI data-collection mechanisms include patient satisfaction surveys, employee satisfaction surveys, financial analyses, occurrence reports, and reports of concern. CPI can help programs collaborate more effectively with external partners, enhance quality of care and service delivery, improve job satisfaction for health care personnel, and establish more-efficient processes (Chestatee Regional Hospital, 2017).

On the other hand, CQI is a management philosophy that seeks to enhance the quality of services and products though process improvement and performance measurement. In the health care realm, CQI is the process-oriented approach for enhancing the quality of treatment and services through regular data collection and analysis (Mittman & Salem-Schatz, 2012). A couple of examples of CQI implementation offer insights that might improve WBV processes and outcomes. These examples could also apply to the other entities (CVN, WCN, Headstrong, etc.) that deliver mental health services.

The first example comes from VHA, which has sought to leverage CQI through research and data-driven efforts, such as the Quality Enhancement Research Initiative (QUERI) (National Academy of Public Administration, 2008). QUERI seeks to improve VHA processes and enhance veterans' health outcomes by quickly integrating effective, evidence-based practices into regular clinical care (Quality Enhancement Research Initiative, 2015). The individual nongovernmental organizations within the veteran mental health system of systems may benefit from such systematic evaluation of their individual processes and rapid integration of evidence-based practices to improve quality and performance.

In addition to QUERI, the VHA has developed Evidence-Based Quality Improvement, a multilevel approach for supporting organizational change and innovation spread (Rubenstein et al., 2014). This approach incorporates bottom-up local innovation and spread within the context of top-down organizational priorities. Multidisciplinary stakeholders participate at the local and regional levels to design innovations using CQI through clinical partnerships. Use of this approach in redesigning a veteran mental health system of systems would help support collaboration and integration within and across silos to achieve the desired goals of a successful partnership.

A second example of CQI implementation that may be helpful for the veteran mental health systems is the lean management approach. Based on the Toyota Production System and a derivative of CQI, the lean management approach emphasizes client value while reducing unnecessary complexity in work processes (Jaworski, 2017). In its health care application, some key elements of the lean approach are aligning front-line staff with the program's performance objectives, developing staff members as problem solvers so that they can make continuous improvements, creating workflows with flexible regimentation, and training leadership to coach staff teams (Jaworski, 2017). This approach is increasingly being used in the health care sector with the goal of consolidating services through coordination of those services within a network to increase efficiency (Gaynor and Town, 2012; Baker, Bundorf, & Kessler, 2014; White and Egouchi, 2014).

Integrating strategies from CPI and CQI may help improve efficiency and effectiveness across the existing nongovernmental veteran mental health systems. Many of the WBV/WCN grantees have taken steps to implement CPI, using patient satisfaction surveys, financial analysis, and other reports on their processes. However, all organizations can do more to take regular account of their performance and adjust processes accordingly. In addition, grantees have integrated some elements of CQI into their management techniques. WBV grantees and other networks could also benefit from adopting additional aspects of CQI, including streamlining processes and linking staff members and activities with specified performance goals.

The WBV grantees are continuously collecting data on their activities and regularly assessing their impact and their direction as they compose performance reports for funders and internal analysis. It is not clear to what extent they have uniformly sought to implement the regular, front-line–level empowerment of personnel to assess processes and quality and make adjustments. Insights from grantees' continuous assessment and adaptation should be shared across the initiative. Furthermore, the incremental, collaborative assessments and shifts in processes will help grantees avoid the need to make less-informed radical shifts in strategy and practices to sustain their programs. The same could hold true for other nongovernmental networks of veteran mental health care.

Adapting Based on Lessons Learned

Through assessing lessons learned and best practices established by other programs and systems of care, WBV grantees and other organizations in the veteran mental health system can adapt to processes and structure that will better align them as a system of systems. VHA and MHS have made substantial improvements in the quality of care that they provide by making adjustments to management and processes (Kilpatrick, Best, Smith, Kudler, & Cornelison-Grant, 2011). By making changes based on VHA and MHS lessons learned, WBV and other private networks may also see enhanced quality of care (Kilpatrick, Best, Smith, Kudler, & Cornelison-Grant, 2011). Specifically, cultivating a collaborative and client-centered culture and establishing and refining technologies that facilitate enhanced communication and coordination are two ways in which WBV can learn from developments in the field.

Adopting a Culture of Collaboration and Client-Centered Care

While the individual WBV clinical sites all report that they develop individually tailored treatment approaches that are often problem-focused, WBV grantees and other organizations can learn a lot about how to function within a system of systems from the broader veterans' health care field. For example, the *no-wrong-door* approach is one way in which VA has integrated its internal programs. Essentially, this approach within the MyVA initiative aims to ensure that veterans will not come to a "wrong door" in seeking services and will receive helpful guidance on the services they need regardless of the point of contact within the network of services (National Academy of Public Administration, 2008). The no-wrong-door system of care is an integrated network of community services that supports clients in navigating various benefits and services (Altarum Institute, n.d.).

VA's organizational values reflect aspects of both the no-wrong-door approach and lean management. The MyVA Initiative instituted VA's organizational values—integrity, commitment, advocacy, respect, and excellence (ICARE)—which seek to ensure that every VA employee approaches their work with deep consideration of the veterans it affects. As promoted in the no-wrong-door approach, these values guide VA employees to help veterans get the care and benefits they are seeking regardless of whether the employees are directly responsible for the services the veterans need. Like the lean management approach, the ICARE values encourage VA employees to solve problems to connect veterans with the care and benefits they are seeking. WBV and the other networks all report being veteran-centric and having mechanisms in place for referring veterans to other support services and supports when necessary. However, these networks may benefit from adopting an ethos that promotes veteran-centered care and the ICARE values, particularly as networks work to align and integrate with each other.

Develop Technologies for Improved Communication and Coordination

Information and communications technologies are critical to sharing data and coordinating within an effective system of systems (Wickramasinghe, Chalasani, Boppana, & Madni, 2007). E-health and electronic medical records sharing will be critical to future development of a robust system of systems for service members, veterans, and families' mental health care (Wickramasinghe, Chalasani, Boppana, & Madni, 2007). Various systems of care have focused on improving technologies that enhance collaboration. For example, VHA has struggled with implementation of its electronic medical record sharing through use of the Veteran Lifetime Electronic Record initiative, but the agency continues to focus on improving the platform (Hosek & Straus 2013). Furthermore, VHA and MHS have also faced challenges with information exchange (GAO , 2015b), but the agencies have established interoperable EHR systems that they are continuing to develop (Sullivan, 2015). And, more recently, the Secretary of VA announced that the VHA would adopt the MHS medical record.

While this should help improve communication and coordination between VHA and MHS, technical developments are needed for these agencies to more efficiently and effectively partner with private organizations, including new privately funded networks. VHA is working to improve its standard operating procedures for purchasing care from contracted community providers (Greenberg et al., 2015). In addition, through development and continued refinement of the Defense Healthcare Management Systems, MHS is seeking to modernize its electronic medical record system and improve medical data sharing with both VHA and the private sector (Defense Healthcare Management System, Program Executive Office, 2017). As MHS and VHA make progress in bringing the MHS system to the VHA, the agencies must integrate private providers into their systems through connecting technological platforms and establishing and adhering to standard operating procedures for sharing medical records and communicating about patient needs.

Networks Should Enhance Collaboration, Client-Centered Care, and Technological Systems

WBV and the other networks should continue to adapt practices based on the successes and failures of other programs—both inside and outside their own organizations. Learning and adaptation is an area in which WBV shines. In fact, WBV grantees have been exceptionally adaptive and receptive to ideas for improving processes and management. However, grantees can do more to maximize the benefits of this practice. To facilitate such adoption of best practices, WBV grantees and the other networks must continue to communicate openly and regularly about processes and progress toward their shared goals.

Considering some of the best practices from VA may be particularly beneficial for WBV and the other networks. For example, the no-wrong-door approach may be helpful in ensuring that service members, veterans, and families get care even if it is outside one of the individual organizations within these systems. Establishing robust referral mechanisms across these networks will help ensure that service members, veterans, and families do not fall through the cracks and help bolster the strength of local care networks. Furthermore, the ICARE approach is a helpful model for WBV and other systems in their empowerment of personnel to solve problems.

As MHS and VHA work to improve their online platforms for collaboration and information-sharing, private networks, including the WBV, should also enhance their technological systems for such exchange. Opportunities for collaboration with VHA and MHS are auspicious means for sustaining WBV and other private networks. All parties could proactively update their technical systems and standard operating procedures to ensure compatibility as community care partners. In addition, building and maintaining technical systems that facilitate information-tracking and information-sharing will help WBV grantees and other private networks monitor their own performance and make adjustments through CPI and CQI. Technology-facilitated information gathering and sharing will also help grantees communicate with each other, with funders, and with other key stakeholders.

Focusing on the Greater Good

One key aspect of the system-of-systems approach is effectively leveraging competition in health care systems and the programs within it. Michael E. Porter, Bishop William Lawrence University Professor at Harvard Business School, has pointed to zero-sum competition as a major issue in the U.S. health care system. In zero-sum competition, programs within systems compete with each other for resources because one program's gain is another's loss (Wickramasinghe, Chalasani, Boppana, & Madni, 2007). Porter recommends reframing health care systems to promote positive-sum competition (Wickramasinghe, Chalasani, Boppana, & Madni, 2007), which would reorient competition toward improving treatments and offering value-driven and patient-centered care (Porter, 2004). Positive-sum competition focuses health care programs' rivalry on offering the best-value treatment and services to attract and retain patients. Positive-sum competition is developed through building distinct programs that offer specialized expertise and personalized services, simplify billing, make pricing of care more transparent, and provide better access to information about providers and health care programs so that patients can make informed decisions about their medical care (Porter, 2004).

Orienting WBV Efforts Toward Positive-Sum Competition

To reorient WBV and the other networks toward positive sum competition, individual WBV grantees and private network clinical partners may need to reconceptualize their missions and how they demonstrate their value. Each organization may need to create or refine its mission in a manner that more explicitly acknowledges that its efforts contribute to the greater mental health care environment. In addition, to establish collaborative efforts that are mutually focused on improving service and quality, organizations (grantees and others across the other networks) must instill a culture of collaboration and promote specified objectives for coordinating in the broader mental health landscape. Examples of objectives aimed at improving coordination within the greater system of systems include establishing and developing partnerships, working with partners to adapt processes and develop new initiatives and strategies, sharing best practices and lessons learned, communicating regularly with other stakeholders within the field, and making referrals to partner organizations.

In addition, sharing best practices and lessons learned may take away one grantee's competitive edge but improve efficiency and effectiveness across the initiative and the larger mental health field. If programs' shared mission is to improve the mental health of service members, veterans, and their families, then the need to collaborate and invest in the greater good is axiomatic. The Institute for Healthcare Improvement's Breakthrough Series Collaboratives uses a group "learning session" approach to facilitate service improvement. These learning sessions typically involve three face-to-face meetings over the course of 12- to 18-month collaboratives and monthly telephone calls in which key members of quality improvement teams meet regularly to share innovations (Institute for Healthcare Improvement, 2003). This iterative process facilitates improved goal-setting in three action phases: adapt and test improvement strategies, further refine improvement strategies and begin spreading successful changes throughout the organization, and adopt successful changes throughout the organization. All of this is conducted with ongoing support from experts on organizational change and content. Such an effort could be tailored for the purposes of creating a system of systems to improve the care of veterans and their families; to be most successful, however, these approaches will need to be resourced and staffed to ensure that efforts are maintained.

Achieving Long-Term Sustainability

A main dimension of the complexity of a system-of-systems approach is the uncertainty of the future of the systems and programs within it (DeLaurentis & Callaway, 2004). Likewise, public-private partnerships offer additional, supplementary routes to mental health care for service members, veterans, and their families, but it is unclear how private programs will maintain funding and relationships within the greater system of care in the long term. Many private mental health providers, such as WBV, WCN, and CVN and other nonprofit organizations, rely on grants from public organizations and philanthropic funders to sustain services and activities. The extent of philanthropic support may not be sustainable in the long term if public interest in service members, veterans, and families changes and/or other issues take priority. Funding for grants from public organizations is also susceptible to shifts in priorities and resources (Carter & Kidder, 2015).

In addition, building and maintaining relationships between programs can also be a challenge. Finding time, resources, and motivation for collaboration can be difficult because the nature of mental health care is intensive and because the demand for care is high. Moreover, administrative barriers to institutionalizing referral processes and information-sharing can hinder collaboration. Despite these challenges, fostering these relationships is critical to the sustainability of individual grantees and the success of the initiative.

Planning Activities for Long-Term Sustainability

Strategic planning for these systems is needed to build the appropriate infrastructure and make the arrangements and investments to support public-private partnerships in the long term. The sustainability of each system is contingent on the organizations' institutionalization of their partnerships. In fact, networking with other program stakeholders can provide a means of learning about sustainability initiatives that are working elsewhere and that may have potential in other areas. Adopting lessons from the corporate social responsibility literature, thinking strategically about maximizing the value to stakeholders, and developing measures of shared value can help build long-term sustainability (Maltz, Thompson, & Ringold, 2011). Shifting away from reliance on grants from philanthropic and public organizations may also facilitate adoption of positive-sum competition. However, before grantees and organizations can make transformational changes to their individual sustainability models, they must position themselves to contribute meaningfully to the overall system. Furthermore, given the broader shifts in the military and veterans' health care systems toward the use of new technology, greater reliance on community providers, and other methods of overcoming barriers to care, grantees must establish a collective culture of learning and performance management to continue to adjust their methods and strategies as the systems of care evolve.

Conclusion

The military and veteran systems of care are complex. There are numerous options for accessing care, and service members, veterans, and their families may use different programs sequentially or concurrently as circumstances change. In addition, the processes for mental health care provision are changing, and MHS and VHA are increasingly reliant on community care to meet their missions. WBV and newer initiatives on the horizon have the opportunity to improve mental health care for service members, veterans, and families through their efforts to provide direct services and to train community providers in military culture competency; evidence-based practices; and other knowledge, skills, and abilities.

The military and veterans' mental health care landscape reflects both adaptation and stagnation in the face of enduring challenges. Although there are a number of changes in the military and veterans' policy environment, particularly with respect to the capacity of the VA to meet the demands of all veterans and their families, there are also many continuing issues (such as workforce development) that all entities within the systems of care continue to work to address. As nongovernmental sources of mental health care for veterans and their families continue to expand and evolve, addressing the issues with sustainability and dependence on philanthropy will be vital. As some entities work toward negotiating third-party payments, they can also help create long-term sustainability efforts by focusing on greater coordination and integration—by growing their collaborative networks, institutionalizing partnerships, and improving their technical platforms to enhance communication and compatibility with other systems of care.

In addition to efforts to improve WBV's ability to navigate the external landscape of programs and policies, there are several actions that the nongovernmental sector providers can take to enhance internal processes and management to spur their organizations to function more collaboratively. To boost the quality and reach of services, the community-based nonprofit organizations within the veteran mental health system may benefit from adopting a system-of-systems approach. Better integrating CPI and CQI into activities would allow organizations to adapt more quickly and more responsively to data and on-the-ground practices. Sharing experiences and information across the organizations will help all sites improve their processes and their contributions to the broader mental health care field. In addition, developing new and existing public-private partnerships will help organizations to sustain their programs and extend impact.

Last, thinking about the greater good—beyond the interests of any individual organization—will position the WBV, WCN, CVN, Headstrong, and others to focus on fulfilling a role in the broader veteran mental health care field. Ultimately, the extent to which systems and the programs within them decide to function as a system of systems will expand or limit their long-term sustainability and their impact on service members, veterans, and families' mental health and will help ". . . build an integrated network of support capable of providing effective mental health services for veterans, service members, and their families" (Obama, 2012).

References

Acosta, J. D., Becker, A., Cerully, J. L., Fisher, M. P., Martin, L. T., Vardavas, R., Slaughter, M. E., & Schell, T. L. (2016). *Assessing the Department of Defense's approach to reducing mental health stigma.* Santa Monica, CA: RAND Corporation, RB-9881-OSD. Retrieved from https://www.rand.org/pubs/research_briefs/RB9881.html

Acosta, J. D., Becker, A., Cerully, J. L., Fisher, M. P., Martin, L. T., Vardavas, R., Slaughter, M. E., & Schell, T. L. (2014). *Mental health stigma in the military.* Santa Monica, CA: RAND Corporation, RR-426-OSD. Retrieved from https://www.rand.org/pubs/research_reports/RR426.html

Adler, N. E., Glymour, M. M., & Fielding, J. (2016). Addressing social determinants of health and health inequalities. *Journal of the American Medical Association, 316,* 1641–1642.

Albin, A. (2016, April 13). UCLA Operation Mend launches mental health program for wounded veterans and their families. *UCLA Newsroom.* Retrieved from http://newsroom.ucla.edu/releases/ucla-operation-mend-launches-mental-health-program-for-wounded-veterans-and-their-families

Altarum Institute. (n.d.). *No wrong door for our nation's vets.* Retrieved from http://altarum.org/our-work/no-wrong-door-for-our-nation%E2%80%99s-vets#sthash.T7NuCeLg.dpuf

America's Warrior Partnership. (n.d.). *About us.* Retrieved from https://americaswarriorpartnership.org/about/

AmericaServes. (n.d.-a). *AmericaServes.* Retrieved from http://americaserves.org

AmericaServes. (n.d.-b). *AmericaServes locations.* Retrieved from http://americaserves.org/veterans/americaserves-locations

American Hospital Association. (2012, January). Bringing behavioral health into the care continuum: opportunities to improve quality, costs and outcomes. *Trend Watch.* Washington, DC: Avalere. Retrieved from http://www.aha.org/research/reports/tw/12jan-tw-behavhealth.pdf

American Psychological Association (n.d.). *The critical need for mental health professionals trained to treat post-traumatic stress disorder and traumatic brain injury.* Retrieved from http://www.apa.org/about/gr/issues/military/critical-need.aspx

Ani, C., Bazargan, M., Hindman, D. Bell,D., Farooq, M. A., Akhanjee, L., Yemofio, F., Baker, R., & Rodriguez, M. (2008). Depression symptomatology and diagnosis: Discordance between patients and physicians in primary care settings. *BMC Family Practice, 9.*

Bagalman, E. (2014). The number of veterans that use VA health care services: a fact sheet. Washington, DC: Congressional Research Service.

Baker, L. C., Bundorf, M. K., & Kessler, D. P. (2014). Vertical integration: Hospital ownership of physician practices is associated with higher prices and spending. *Health Affairs, 35*, 756–763.

Bititci, U. S., Martinez, V., Albores, P. & Parung, J. (2004). Creating and managing value in collaborative networks. *International Journal of Physical Distribution & Logistics Management, 34*, 251–268.

Brink, S. (2014, April 29). Mental health now covered under ACA, but not for everyone. *US News & World Report.* Retrieved from http://www.usnews.com/news/articles/2014/04/29/mental-health-now-covered-under-aca-but-not-for-everyone

Brown, R. A., Marshall, G. N., Breslau, J., Farris, C., Osilla, K. C., Pincus, H. A., Ruder, T., Voorhies, P., Barnes-Proby, D., Pfrommer, K., Miyashiro, L., Yashodhara, R., & Adamson, D. M. (2015). *Improving access to behavioral health care for remote service members and their families.* Santa Monica, CA: RAND Corporation, RR-578/1-OSD. Retrieved from https://www.rand.org/pubs/research_reports/RR578z1.html

Burnam, M. A., Meredith, L. S., Tanielian, T., & Jaycox, L. H. (2009). Mental health care for Iraq and Afghanistan war veterans. *Health Affairs, 28*, 771–782.

Byrne, C. A., & Riggs, D. S. (1996). The cycle of trauma: Relationship aggression in male Vietnam veterans with symptoms of posttraumatic stress disorder. *Violence and Victims, 11*, 213–225.

Carter, P. (2012). *Upholding the promise: Supporting veterans and military personnel in the next four years.* Washington, DC: Center for a New American Security.

Carter, P., & Kidder, K. (2015, September 9). *Charting the sea of goodwill.* Washington, DC: Center for a New American Security. Retrieved from https://www.cnas.org/publications/reports/charting-the-sea-of-goodwill

Chairman's Office of Reintegration: Veterans/Families/Communities. (2014). *After the sea of goodwill: A collective approach to veteran reintegration.* Washington, DC: Office of the Chairman of the Joint Chiefs of Staff. Retrieved from http://www.jcs.mil/Portals/36/Documents/CORe/After_the_Sea_of_Goodwill.pdf

Chestatee Regional Hospital. (2017). *Continuous performance improvement.* (No longer working.) Retrieved from http://www.chestateeregionalhospital.com/getpage.php?name=neo8

Collins, C., Hewson, D. L., Munger, R. & Wade, T. (2010). *Evolving models of behavioral health integration in primary care.* New York: Milbank Memorial Fund.

Colton, C. W., & Manderscheid, R. W. (2006). Congruencies in increased mortality rates, years of potential life lost, and causes of death among public mental health clients in eight states. *Preventing Chronic Disorders, 3*, A42.

DeLaurentis, D., & Callaway, R. K. (2004). A system-of-systems perspective for public policy decisions. *Review of Policy Research, 21*, 829–837.

Defense Healthcare Management System, Program Executive Office. (2017, July 13). Understanding the defense healthcare management systems program executive office landscape [fact sheet]. Washington, DC: U.S. Department of Defense. Retrieved from https://health.mil/Reference-Center/Fact-Sheets/2017/08/02/Understanding-the-Defense-Healthcare-Management-Systems-Program-Executive-Office-Landscape

DoD—*See* U.S. Department of Defense.

Duke Evidence-Based Practice Implementation Center. (2015). *Welcome Back Veterans Initiative.* (No longer working.) Retrieved from http://epic.psychiatry.duke.edu/projects/welcome-back-veterans

Embrey, E. P. (2009, September 18). Policy Memorandum Implementation of the 'Patient-Centered Medical Home' Model of Primary Care in MTFs [memorandum]. Washington, DC: Office of the Assistant Secretary of Defense, Deputy Assistant Secretary of Defense (Force Health Protection and Readiness).

Emory Healthcare. (n.d.-a). *Welcome to the Emory healthcare veterans program.* Retrieved from http://emoryhealthcare.org/veterans-program/index.html

Emory Healthcare. (n.d.-b) *Military sexual trauma (MST).* Retrieved from http://emoryhealthcare.org/veterans-program/conditions/mst.html

Engel, C. C. (2014). Compromised confidentiality is harmful: military owes proof to the contrary. *Psychiatric Times, 31,* 30.

Fulton, K., Kasper, G., & Kibbe, B. (2010, July). *What's next for philanthropy: Acting bigger and adapting better in a networked world.* San Francisco, CA: Monitor Institute. Retrieved from http://monitorinstitute.com/downloads/what-we-think/whats-next/Whats_Next_for_Philanthropy.pdf

Funk, M., Lund, C., Freeman, M. & Drew, N. (2009). Improving the quality of mental health care. *International Journal for Quality in Health Care, 21,* 415–420.

GAO—See U.S. Government Accountability Office.

Gaynor, M., & Town, R. (2012). *The impact of hospital consolidation—update.* Washington, D.C.: Robert Wood Johnson Foundation Synthesis Report.

George W. Bush Institute. (2017, February 24). *Warrior Wellness Alliance: Addressing the invisible wounds of war.* Retrieved from http://www.bushcenter.org/publications/resources-reports/reports/invisible-wounds.html

Give an Hour. (n.d.-a). *About us.* Retrieved from https://giveanhour.org/about-give-an-hour/

Give an Hour. (n.d.-b). *Guided provider search.* Retrieved from https://www.giveanhour.org/GettingHelp/GuidedProviderSearch.aspx

Gondek, D., Edbrooke-Childs, J., Velikonja, T., Chapman, L., Saunders, F., Hayes D., & Wolpert, M. (2017). Facilitators and barriers to person-centred care in child and young people mental health services: A systematic review. *Clinical Psychology & Psychotherapy, 24,* 870–886.

Gordon, A. L. (2016, April 7). Steven Cohen pledges $275 million to veteran mental health care. *Bloomberg* (subscription only).

Gordon, S. (2016, January 28). How VA health care outdoes the private sector. *Beyond Chron.* Retrieved from http://www.beyondchron.org/31264-2/

Gorman, G. H., Eide, M., & Hisle-Gorman, E. (2010). Wartime military deployment and increased pediatric mental and behavioral health complaints. *Pediatrics, 126,* 1058–1066.

Gray, L. C., Berg, K., Fries, B. E., Henrard, J.-C., Hirdes, J. P., Steel, K.,& Morris, J. N. (2009). Sharing clinical information across care settings: The birth of an integrated assessment system. *BMC Health Services Research, 9,* 71.

Greenberg, M. D., Batka, C., Buttorff, C., Dunigan, M., Lovejoy, S. L., McGovern, G., Pace, N. M., Pillemer, F., Williams, K. M., Apaydin, E., Aranibar, C., Buenaventura, M., Carter, P., Cherney, S., Davis, L. E., Donohue, A. G., Geyer, L., Fleming, J., Roshan, P., Skrabala, L., Simmons, S., Thompson, J., Welch, J., Hosek S. D., & Farmer, C. M. (2015). *Authorities and mechanisms for purchased care at the Department of Veterans Affairs.* Santa Monica, CA: RAND Corporation, RR1165/3-VA. Retrieved from https://www.rand.org/pubs/research_reports/RR1165z3.html

Gugliotta, G. (2013, April 7). VA drive to hire 1,600 mental health professionals hits community clinics' supply. *Kaiser Health News.* Retrieved from http://khn.org/news/va-hiring-mental-health-professionals-impact-on-community-health-centers/

Heal, A. (2000). *Mental health and work: Impact, issues and good practices.* Geneva, Switzerland: World Health Organization.

Henry J. Kaiser Family Foundation. (2016, December 31). *Mental health care health professional shortage areas (HPSAs).* Retrieved from http://kff.org/other/state-indicator/mental-health-care-health-professional-shortage-areas-hpsas/

Hepner, K. A., Farris, C., Farmer, C. M., Iyiewuare, P. O., Tanielian, T., Wilks, A., Robbins, M., Paddock, S. M., & Pincus, H. A. (2017). *Delivering clinical practice guideline–concordant care for PTSD and major depression in military treatment facilities.* Santa Monica, CA: RAND Corporation. RR-1692-OSD. Retrieved from https://www.rand.org/pubs/research_reports/RR1692.html

Hepner, K. A., Roth, C. P., Sloss, E. M., Paddock, S. M., Iyiewuare, P. O., Timmer, M. J., & Pincus, H. A. (2017). *Quality of care for PTSD and depression in the military health system: Final report.* Santa Monica, CA: RAND Corporation, RR-1542-OSD. Retrieved from https://www.rand.org/pubs/research_reports/RR1542.html

Hepner, K. A., Sloss, E. M., Roth, C. P., Krull, H., Paddock, S. M., Moen, S. Timmer M. J., & Pincus, H. A. (2016) *Quality of care for PTSD and depression in the military health system: Phase I report.* Santa Monica, CA: RAND Corporation, RR-978-OSD. Retrieved from https://www.rand.org/pubs/research_reports/RR978.html

Hoge, C. W., Auchterlonie, J. L., & Milliken, C. S. (2006). Mental health problems, use of mental health services, and attrition from military service after returning from deployment to Iraq or Afghanistan. *Journal of the American Medical Association, 295,* 1023–1032.

Hoge, C. W., Castro, C. A., Messer, S. C., McGurk, D., Cotting, D. I., & Koffman, R. L. (2004). Combat duty in Iraq and Afghanistan, mental health problems, and barriers to care. *New England Journal of Medicine, 351,* 13–22.

Hoge, C. W., Ivany, C. G., Brusher, E. A., Brown, M. D. III, Shero, J. C., Adler, A. B., Warner, C. H., & Orman, D. T. (2015). Transformation of mental health care for US soldiers and families during the Iraq and Afghanistan wars: Where science and politics intersect. *American Journal of Psychiatry, 173,* 334–343.

Hoge, C. W., Terhakopian, A., Castro, C. A., Messer, S. C., & Engel, C. C. (2007). Association of posttraumatic stress disorder with somatic symptoms, health care visits, and absenteeism among Iraq war veterans. *American Journal of Psychiatry, 164,* 150–153.

Hogg Foundation for Mental Health and Methodist Healthcare Ministries. (2011). *Crisis point: Mental health workforce shortages in Texas.* Austin, TX: Author.

Holliday, S. B., Pedersen, E. R., & Leventhal, A. M. (2016). Depression, posttraumatic stress, and alcohol misuse in young adult veterans: The transdiagnostic role of distress tolerance. *Drug and Alcohol Dependence, 161,* 348–355.

Home Base Veteran and Family Care. (n.d.). *Family care + support at home base.* Retrieved from http://www.homebase.org/clinical-care/clinical-care-support/

Hosek, S. D., & Straus, S. G. (2013). *Patient privacy, consent, and identity management in health information exchange: Issues for the military health system.* Santa Monica, CA: RAND Corporation, RR-112-A. Retrieved from https://www.rand.org/pubs/research_reports/RR112.html

Hussey, P. S., Ringel, J., Ahluwalia, S. Price, R. A., Buttorff, C., Concannon, T. W., Lovejoy, S. L., Martsolf, G., Rudin, R. S., Schultz, D., Sloss, E. M., Watkins, K. E., Waxman, D., Bauman, M., Briscombe, B., Broyles, J. R., Burns, R. M., Chen, E. K., DeSantis, A. S. J., Ecola, L., Fischer, S. H., Friedberg, M. W., Gidengil, C. A., Ginsburg, P. B., Gulden, T., Gutierrez, C. I., Hirshman, S., Huang, C. Y., Kandrack, R., Kress, A., Leuschner, K., MacCarthy, S., Maksabedian, E. J., Mann, S., Matthews, L. J., May, L. W., Mishra, N., Kraus, L., Muchow, A. N., Nelson, J., Naranjo, D., O'Hanlon, C. E., Pillemer, F., Predmore, Z., Ross, R., Ruder, T., Rutter, C. M., Uscher-Pines, L., Vaiana, M. E., Vesely, J., Hosek, S. D., & Farmer, C. M. (2015). *Resources and Capabilities of the Department of Veterans Affairs to Provide Timely and Accessible Care to Veterans.* Santa Monica, CA: RAND Corporation, RR-1165/2-VA. Retrieved from https://www.rand.org/pubs/research_reports/RR1165z2.html

IHS Markit. (2016). *The complexities of physician supply and demand: Projections from 2014 to 2025.* Washington, D.C.: Association of American Medical Colleges.

Institute for Healthcare Improvement. (2003). *The Breakthrough Series: IHI's collaborative model for achieving breakthrough improvement.* Boston: Author.

Institute of Medicine. (2006). *Improving the quality of health care for mental and substance-use conditions.* Washington, DC: National Academy Press.

Institute of Medicine. (2012). *Treatment for posttraumatic stress disorder in military and veteran populations: Initial assessment.* Washington, DC: National Academies Press.

Institute of Medicine. (2013). *Returning home from Iraq and Afghanistan: Assessment of readjustment needs of veterans, service members, and their families.* Washington, DC: National Academies Press.

IOM—*See* Institute of Medicine.

Jaworski, N. (2017). Building a culture of continuous performance improvement [Briefing]. Ottowa, ONT: Queensway Carleton Hospital.

Jenkins, K. (2014). *Information-sharing in mental health care provision: A review.* London: Mental Health Foundation on behalf of the Strategic Partnership Mental Health Consortia.

Jorm, A. (2000). Mental health literacy: Public knowledge and beliefs about. *British Journal of Psychiatry, 177,* 317–327.

Julian, R. M. (2013). Military Health System (MHS) Patient Centered Medical Home (PCMH) Brief to Recovering Warrior Task Force [Briefing]. Fort Belvoir, VA: TRICARE Management Activity, Office of the Chief Medical Officer.

Kilbourne, A. M., Keyser, D., & Pincus, H. A. (2010). Challenges and opportunities in measuring the quality of mental health care. *Canadian Journal of Psychiatry, 55,* 549–557.

Kilpatrick, D., Best, C., Smith, D., Kudler, H., & Cornelison-Grant, V. (2011). Serving those who have served: Educational needs of health care providers working with military members, veterans, and their families. *A web survey of mental health and primary care professionals.* Charleston, SC: Medical University of South Carolina Department of Psychiatry, National Crime Victims Research & Treatment Center.

Koblinsky, S. A., Leslie, L. A., & Cook, E. T. (2014). Treating behavioral health conditions of OEF/OIF veterans and their families: A state needs assessment of civilian providers. *Military Behavioral Health, 2*, 162-172.

Kuhn, E., Greene, C., Hoffman, J., Nguyen, T., Wald, W., Schmidt, J., . . . & Ruzek, J. (2014). Preliminary Evaluation of PTSD coach, a smartphone app for post-traumatic stress symptoms. *Military Medicine, 179*, 12–18.

M-SPAN—*See* Military Support Programs and Networks.

Maltz, E., Thompson, F., and Ringold, D. J. (2011). Assesing and maximizing corporate social initiatives: A strategic view of corporate social responsibility. *Journal of Public Affairs, 11*, 344–352.

Meadows, S. O., Tanielian, T. L., & Karney, B. R. (Eds.) (2016). *The Deployment Life Study: Longitudinal analysis of military families across the deployment cycle.* Santa Monica, CA: RAND Corporation, RR-1388-A/OSD. Retrieved from https://www.rand.org/pubs/research_reports/RR1388.html

Merlis, M. (2012). *The future of health care for military personnel and veterans.* Washington, DC: Academy Health. Retrieved from http://www.academyhealth.org/files/publications/files/publications/AH%255FRIBriefMilVetsFinal.pdf

Milliken, C. S., Auchterlonie, J. L., & Hoge, C. W. (2007). Longitudinal assessment of mental health problems among active and reserve component soldiers returning from the Iraq war. *Journal of the American Medical Association, 298*, 2141–2148.

Military Health System and Defense Health Agency. (n.d.). *About the Military Health System.* Retrieved from http://www.health.mil/About-MHS

Military Support Programs and Networks. (n.d.-a). *Deployment cycle support.* Retrieved from http://m-span.org/programs-for-military-families/deployment-cycle-support

Military Support Programs and Networks. (n.d.-b). *HomeFront Strong.* Retrieved from http://m-span.org/programs-for-military-families/homefront-strong/

Military Support Programs and Networks. (n.d.-c). *Strong Military Families.* Retrieved from http://m-span.org/our-programs/strong-military-families/

Mittman, B., & Salem-Schatz, S. (2012, December). *Improving research and evaluation around continuous quality improvement in health care.* Washington, DC: Robert Wood Johnson Foundation. Retrieved from http://www.rwjf.org/en/library/research/2012/11/improving-research-and-evaluation-around-continuous-quality-impr.html

M-SPAN—*See* Military Support Programs and Networks.

Murphy, R. A. & Fairbank, J. A. (2013). Implementation and dissemination of military informed and evidence-based interventions for community dwelling military families. *Clinical Child and Family Psychology Review, 16*, 348–364.

National Academy of Public Administration (2008). *After yellow ribbons: Providing veteran-centered services.* Washington, DC: Author.

National Alliance on Mental Illness. (n.d.) *Veterans & active duty.* Retrieved from https://www.nami.org/Find-Support/Veterans-and-Active-Duty

National Center for PTSD. (2015a, August 13). *Effects of PTSD on family.* Retrieved from http://www.ptsd.va.gov/public/family/effects-ptsd-family.asp

National Center for PTSD. (2015b, August 13). *PTSD and substance abuse in veterans.* Retrieved from
http://www.ptsd.va.gov/public/problems/ptsd_substance_abuse_veterans.asp

National Center for PTSD. (2016, October 3). *How common is PTSD?* Retrieved from
http://www.ptsd.va.gov/public/PTSD-overview/basics/how-common-is-ptsd.asp

National Center for PTSD. (2017a, April 11). *Mobile applications.* Retrieved from
http://www.ptsd.va.gov/public/materials/apps/index.asp

National Center for PTSD. (2017b, May 31). *Mobile app: PTSD coach.* Retrieved from
http://www.ptsd.va.gov/public/materials/apps/PTSDCoach.asp

National Coalition for Homeless Veterans. (n.d.) *Background and statistics.* Retrieved from
http://nchv.org/index.php/news/media/background_and_statistics/

National Council for Behavioral Health (2012). *Meeting the behavioral health needs of veterans: Operation Enduring Freedom and Operation Iraqi Freedom.* Washington, DC: Author.

Neuhauser, J. A. (2010). Lives of quiet desperation: The conflict between military necessity and confidentiality. *Creighton Law Review, 44,* 1003–1044.

NYU Langone Health. (n.d.). *Military Family Clinic programs & services.* Retrieved from:
http://nyulangone.org/locations/steven-a-cohen-military-family-clinic/
military-family-clinic-programs-services

NYU Langone Health. (2015, July 16). The Home Depot Foundation awards $1.5 million to NYU Langone Medical Center to help veterans with post-traumatic stress & traumatic brain injury [Press release]. New York: Author.

NYU Langone Medical Center. (2014a, October 30). For returning veterans suffering from both mental health and substance abuse challenges, treatment can be found under one roof. *PR Newswire.*

NYU Langone Medical Center. (2014b, November 9). NYU Langone receives $1 million for Dual Diagnosis Program. *Philanthropy News Digest.*

Obama, Barack. (2012, August 31). *Executive order—Improving access to mental health services for veterans, service members, and military families.* White House, Office of the Press Secretary. Retrieved from
https://obamawhitehouse.archives.gov/the-press-office/2012/08/31/
executive-order-improving-access-mental-health-services-veterans-service

Office of Rural Health. (2014). *Fact Sheet: Information about the VHA Office of Rural Health and Rural Veterans.* Retrieved from
http://www.ruralhealth.va.gov/docs/factsheets/ORH_General_FactSheet_2014.pdf

Office of Rural Health. (2015, January 30). Office of Rural Health: Caring for rural veterans [Video file]. Retrieved from
https://www.youtube.com/watch?v=yyIjKAa-kv0

Panangala, S. V. (2016). *Health care for veterans: answers to frequently asked questions.* Washington, DC: Congressional Research Service.

Parks, J., Svendsen, D., Singer, P., Foti, M. E., & Mauer, B. (2006, October). *Morbidity and mortality in people with serious mental illness.* Alexandria, VA: National Association of State Mental Health Program Directors (NASMHPD) Medical Directors Council. Retrieved from
http://nasmhpd.org/sites/default/files/
Mortality%20and%20Morbidity%20Final%20Report%208.18.08.pdf

Patient Care Services. (2016, September 22). *Patient Aligned Care Team (PACT)*. Retrieved from http://www.va.gov/health/services/primarycare/pact/index.Asp

Pedersen, E. R., Eberhart, N. K., Williams, K. M., Tanielian, T., Epley, C., & Scharf, D. M. (2015). *Public-private partnerships for providing behavioral health care to veterans and their families: What do we know, what do we need to learn, and what do we need to do?* Santa Monica, CA: RAND Corporation, RR-994-NYSHF/MTF. Retrieved from https://www.rand.org/pubs/research_reports/RR994.html

Plsek, P. (2001). *Crossing the quality chasm: A new health system for the 21st century.* Washington, DC: Institute of Medicine.

Porter, M. E. (2004, July 12). Michael Porter's prescription for the high cost of health care. *Harvard Business School Working Knowledge.* Retrieved from http://hbswk.hbs.edu/item/michael-porters-prescription-for-the-high-cost-of-health-care

Prigerson, H. G., Maciejewski, P. K., & Rosenheck, R. A. (2002). Population attributable fractions of psychiatric disorders and behavioral outcomes associated with combat exposure among US men. *American Journal of Public Health, 92*, 59–63.

Quality Enhancement Research Initiative. (2015, September 16). *About the QUERI program.* Retrieved from http://www.queri.research.va.gov/about/default.cfm

Radnofsky, L. (2015, February 16). Where are the mental-health providers? *Wall Street Journal.*

Ramchand, R., Ahluwalia, S., Xenakis, L., Apaydin, E., Raaen, L., & Grimm, G. (2017). A systematic review of peer-supported interventions for health promotion and disease prevention. *Preventive Medicine, 101*, 156–170.

Ramchand, R., Schell, T. L., Karney, B. R., Osilla, K. C., Burns, R. M., & Caldarone, L. B. (2010). Disparate prevalence estimates of PTSD among service members who served in Iraq and Afghanistan: Possible explanations. *Journal of Traumatic Stress, 23*, 59–68.

Ramchand, R., Tanielian, T., Fisher, M. P., Vaughan, C. A., Trail, T. E., Epley, C., Voorhies, P., Robbins, M. W., Robinson, E., and Ghosh-Dastidar, B. (2014). *Hidden heroes: America's military caregivers.* Santa Monica, CA: RAND Corporation, RR-499-TEDF. Retrieved from https://www.rand.org/pubs/research_reports/RR499.html

Richardson, S., & Asthana, S. (2006). Inter-agency information sharing in health and social care services: The role of professional culture. *British Journal of Social Work, 36*, 657–669.

Road Home Program. (n.d.). *Help for traumatic brain injury.* Retrieved from http://roadhomeprogram.org/veteran-mental-health-services/traumatic-brain-injury/

Rosland, A.-M., Nelson, K., Sun, H., Dolan, E. D., Maynard, C., Bryson, C., Stark, R., . . . Fihn, S. D. (2013). The patient-centered medical home in the Veterans Health Administration. *American Journal of Managed Care, 19*, e263–e272.

Rouse, Margaret. (2012, February 20). System of systems (SoS). *Tech Target.* Retrieved from http://searchsoa.techtarget.com/definition/System-of-systems-SoS

Rubenstein, L. V., Stockdale, S. E., Sapir, N., Altman, L. Dresselhaus, T., Salem-Schatz, S. . . . & Yano, E. M. (2014, July). A patient-centered primary care practice approach using evidence-based quality improvement: Rationale, methods, and early assessment of implementation. *Journal of General Internal Medicine, 29*(2), 589–597. Retrieved from http://link.springer.com/article/10.1007%2Fs11606-013-2703-y

Runge, C. E., Waller, M., MacKenzie, A., & McGuire, A. C. (2014). Spouses of military members' experiences and insights: Qualitative analysis of responses to an open-ended question in a survey of health and wellbeing. *PLOS ONE, 9,* e114755.

Russell, L. (2010). *Mental health care services in primary care: Tackling the issues in the context of health care reform.* Washington, DC: Center for American Progress.

SBHP—*See* Star Behavioral Health Providers.

Schnurr, P. P., & Green, B. L. (2004). *Trauma and health, physical health consequences of exposure to extreme stress.* Washington, DC: American Psychological Association.

Seal, K. H., Bertenthal, D., Miner, C. R., Sen, S., and Marmar, C. (2007). Bringing the war back home: Mental health disorders among 103,788 US veterans returning from Iraq and Afghanistan seen at Department of Veterans Affairs Facilities. *Archives of Internal Medicine, 167,* 476–482.

Seal, K. H., Metzler, T. J., Gima, K. S., Bertenthal, D., Maguen, S. & Marmar, C. R. (2009). Trends and risk factors for mental health diagnoses among Iraq and Afghanistan veterans using Department of Veterans Affairs health care, 2002–2008. *American Journal of Public Health, 99,* 1651–1658.

Soule, A. (2016, April 6). SAC's Cohen pledges $275M to vets for free mental health services. *Stamford Advocate.*

South Central Veterans Integrated Service Network 16, Mental Illness Research, Education, and Clinical Center Consumer Guide Workgroup, Sullivan, G., Arlinghaus, K., Edlund, C., & Kauth, M. (2011, January). *Guide to VA mental health services for veterans & families.* Washington, DC: U.S. Department of Veterans Affairs. Retrieved from https://www.mentalhealth.va.gov/docs/ Guide_to_VA_Mental_Health_Srvcs_FINAL12-20-10.pdf

Star Behavioral Health Providers. (n.d.-a). Retrieved from http://www.starproviders.org

Star Behavioral Health Providers. (n.d.-b). *Tier One.* Retrieved from https://starproviders.org/providers/states/michigan/tier-1-page-id-12

Star Behavioral Health Providers. (n.d.-c). *Tier Two.* Retrieved from https://starproviders.org/providers/states/michigan/tier-2-page-id-13

Star Behavioral Health Providers. (n.d.-d). *Tier Three.* Retrieved from https://starproviders.org/providers/states/michigan/tier-3-page-id-14

Substance Abuse and Mental Health Services Administration. (2014, September 29). *Veterans and military families.* Retrieved from http://www.samhsa.gov/veterans-military-families

Sullivan, T. (2015, July 30). DoD: New EHR not about interoperability with VA. *Healthcare IT News.* Retrieved from http://www.healthcareitnews.com/news/dod-new-ehr-not-about-interoperability-va

Tanielian, T., Farris, C., Epley, C., Farmer, C. M., Robinson, E., Engel, C. C., Robbins, M., & Jaycox, L. H. (2014). *Ready to serve: Community-based provider capacity to deliver culturally competent, quality mental health care to veterans and their families.* Santa Monica, CA: RAND Corporation, RR-806-UNHF. Retrieved from https://www.rand.org/pubs/research_reports/RR806.html

Tanielian, T., & Jaycox, L. H. (2008). *Invisible wounds of war: Psychological and cognitive injuries, their consequences, and services to assist recovery.* Santa Monica, CA: RAND Corporation, MG-720-CCF. Retrieved from https://www.rand.org/pubs/monographs/MG720.html

Tanielian, T., Karney, B. R., Chandra, A., & Meadows, S. O. (2014). *The deployment life study: Methodological overview and baseline sample description.* Santa Monica, CA: RAND Corporation, RR-209-A/OSD. Retrieved from https://www.rand.org/pubs/research_reports/RR209.html

Tanielian, T., Martin, L. T., & Epley, C. (2014). *Enhancing capacity to address mental health needs of veterans and their families: The Welcome Back Veterans initiative.* Santa Monica, CA: RAND Corporation, RR-719-MTF. Retrieved from https://www.rand.org/pubs/research_reports/RR719.html

Tanielian, T., Woldetsadik, M. A., Jaycox, L. H., Batka, C., Moen, S., Farmer, C., & Engel, C. C. (2016). Barriers to engaging service members in mental health care within the U.S. military health system. *Psychiatric Services, 67,* 718–727.

TRICARE. (2016a, November 8). *Information for providers.* Retrieved from http://tricare.mil/providers.aspx

TRICARE. (2016b, December 1). *Eligibility.* Retrieved from http://www.tricare.mil/eligibility

UCLA NFRC—*See* University of California, Los Angeles, Nathanson Family Resilience Center.

Under Secretary of Defense for Personnel and Readiness. (2015, April 17). DoD/VA report to the Congress in response to Senate Report 113-44, pg. 133, accompanying S. 1197, the National Defense Authorization Act for Fiscal Year 2014: Mental health counselors for service members, veterans, and their families. Washington, DC: U.S. Department of Defense and U.S. Department of Veterans Affairs.

University of California, Los Angeles, Nathanson Family Resilience Center. (n.d.-a). *Female veterans initiative.* Retrieved from https://nfrc.ucla.edu/WomenVets

University of California, Los Angeles, Nathanson Family Resilience Center. (n.d.-b). *FOCUS—Early childhood for military and veteran families.*

University of Michigan. (n.d.). *Military Family Support Forum.* Retrieved from http://outreach.umich.edu/programs/military-family-support-forum-mfsf/

U.S. Department of Defense. (2015, February 28). *Evaluation of the TRICARE program: Access, cost, and quality—Fiscal year 2015 report to Congress.* Washington, DC: Author.

U.S. Department of Defense. (2016, March). *TRICARE® mental health care services* [Fact sheet]. Washington, DC: Author.

U.S. Department of Veterans Affairs (n.d.). Eligibility for and enrollment in VA healthcare. *Mental health services: Enrolling in VA healthcare.* Washington, DC: Author. Retrieved from http://www.mentalhealth.va.gov/communityproviders/docs/Eligibility_Criteria.pdf

U.S. Department of Veterans Affairs. (2007). *Fiscal Year 2008 Budget Estimate: 2008 Congressional Submission—Volume 1 Medical Programs.*

U.S. Department of Veterans Affairs. (2008). *FY 2009 president's budget request.*

U.S. Department of Veterans Affairs. (2009). *FY 2010 president's budget request.*

U.S. Department of Veterans Affairs. (2010). *FY 2011 president's budget request.*

U.S. Department of Veterans Affairs. (2011). *FY 2012 president's budget request.*

U.S. Department of Veterans Affairs. (2013, November 5). VA meets president's mental health executive order hiring goal [Blog post]. Retrieved from http://www.blogs.va.gov/VAntage/10793/ va-meets-president's-mental-health-executive-order-hiring-goal/

U.S. Department of Veterans Affairs. (2015). *Department of Veterans Affairs FY 2014–2020 strategic plan.* Retrieved from http://www.va.gov/op3/docs/strategicplanning/va2014-2020strategicplan.pdf

U.S. Department of Veterans Affairs. (2017). *Department of Veterans Affairs—Budget in brief 2017.* Retrieved from https://www.yumpu.com/en/document/view/55986108/ department-of-veterans-affairs-budget-in-brief-2017

U.S. Government Accountability Office. (2015a, October). *VA mental health: Clearer guidance on access policies and wait-time data needed.* Washington, DC: Author.

U.S. Government Accountability Office. (2015b, November 19). *Health: DOD and VA electronic health records systems.* Retrieved from http://www.gao.gov/duplication/action_tracker/ DOD_and_VA_Electronic_Health_Records_Systems/action1

VA—*See* U.S. Department of Veterans Affairs.

VA Mental Health. (n.d.). *Community provider toolkit.* Retrieved from http://www.mentalhealth.va.gov/communityproviders/ index.asp#sthash.UjCpXZvi.hssZnat8.dpbs

Vasterling, J. J., Proctor, S. P., Amoroso, P., Kane, R., Heeren, T., & White, R. F. (2006). Neuropsychological outcomes of army personnel following deployment to the Iraq war. *Journal of the American Medical Association, 296,* 519–529.

Verdeli, H., Baily, C., Vousoura, E., Belser, A., Singla, D. & Manos, G. (2011). The case for treating depression in military spouses. *Journal of Family Psychology, 25,* 488.

Veterans Health Administration. (2015, April 17). *One in ten older vets is depressed.* Retrieved from http://www.va.gov/health/NewsFeatures/20110624a.asp

Veterans Health Administration. (2017, July 13). *About VHA.* Retrieved from http://www.va.gov/health/aboutvha.asp

VHA—*See* Veterans Health Administration.

VISN and MIRECC—*See* South Central Veterans Integrated Service Network 16, Mental Illness Research, Education, and Clinical Center Consumer Guide Workgroup, Sullivan, G., Arlinghaus, K., Edlund, C., & Kauth, M.

Watkins, K. E., Pincus, H. A., Smith, B., Paddock, S. M., Mannle, T. E., Jr., Woodroffe, A., Solomon, J., Sorbero, M. E., Farmer, C. M., Hepner, K. A., Adamson, D. A., Forrest, L., & Call, C. (2011). *Veterans health administration mental health program evaluation: Capstone report.* Santa Monica, CA: RAND Corporation, TR-956-VHA. Retrieved from https://www.rand.org/pubs/technical_reports/TR956.html

Welcome Back Veterans. (2016). *About Welcome Back Veterans.* Retrieved from http://web.welcomebackveterans.org/about/index

White, C., & Egouchi, M. (2014). Reference pricing: A small piece of the health care pricing and quality puzzle. Michigan: National Institute for Health Care Reform, Research Brief No. 18.

Wickramasinghe, N., Chalasani, S., Boppana, R. V., & Madni, A. M. (2007). *Healthcare system of systems*. San Antonio, TX: 2007 IEEE International Conference on System of Systems Engineering.

Wounded Warrior Project. (n.d.). *News media*. Retrieved from https://www.woundedwarriorproject.org/programs/warrior-care-network/news-media.aspx

WWP—*See* Wounded Warrior Project.

Zatzick, D. F., Marmar, C. R., Weiss, D. S., Browner, W. S., Metzler, T. J., Golding, J. M., Stewart, A., Schlenger, W. E., & Wells, K. B. (1997). Posttraumatic stress disorder and functioning and quality of life outcomes in a nationally representative sample of male Vietnam veterans. *American Journal of Psychiatry, 154*, 1690–1695.